George Henry Glasse

Sermons on Various Subjects

more particularly on Christian faith and hope and the consolations of religion

George Henry Glasse

Sermons on Various Subjects
more particularly on Christian faith and hope and the consolations of religion

ISBN/EAN: 9783337100421

Printed in Europe, USA, Canada, Australia, Japan

Cover: Foto ©Lupo / pixelio.de

More available books at **www.hansebooks.com**

SERMONS

ON

VARIOUS SUBJECTS;

MORE PARTICULARLY

ON CHRISTIAN FAITH AND HOPE,

AND

THE CONSOLATIONS OF RELIGION.

BY

GEORGE HENRY GLASSE, M. A.

(LATE STUDENT OF CHRIST-CHURCH, OXFORD)

RECTOR OF HANWELL, MIDDLESEX;

AND CHAPLAIN TO THE RIGHT HONOURABLE

THE EARL OF RADNOR.

LONDON:

PRINTED BY JOHN NICHOLS,

FOR T. CADELL JUNIOR AND W. DAVIES, STRAND.

MDCCXCVIII.

TO MRS. SARAH POTT,

OF DRAYTON-GREEN, NEAR HANWELL, MIDDLESEX,

THE HONOURED RELICT OF PERCIVAL POTT, ESQUIRE,

THESE DISCOURSES,

PREACHED BEFORE HER IN THE PARISH CHURCH OF HANWELL,

AND PUBLISHED SOLELY AT HER REQUEST,

ARE, WITH EVERY SENTIMENT OF ESTEEM AND VENERATION,

HUMBLY DEDICATED,

BY HER MOST OBLIGED AND MOST DEVOTED FRIEND,

GEORGE HENRY GLASSE.

HANWELL RECTORY,
FEBRUARY 26, 1798.

CONTENTS.

SERMON I.
On the Clerical Character.

Titus ii.—7, 8. *In all things shewing thyself a pattern of good works: in doctrine shewing uncorruptness, gravity, sincerity,*
Sound speech, that cannot be condemned; that he that is of the contrary part may be ashamed, having no evil thing to say of you. p. 3.

(First printed A. D. 1794.)

SERMON II.
The Creation.

Genesis i.—1. *In the beginning God created the Heaven and the Earth.* p. 27.

SERMON III.

The Unity of God.

Mark x.—18. *And Jesus said unto him, "Why callest thou me good? There is none good but One: that is, GOD."*

p. 51.

(Preached on Trinity-Sunday.)

SERMON IV.

The Transfiguration.

Luke ix.—29, 30, 31. *And as he prayed, the fashion of his countenance was altered; and his raiment was white and glistering. And behold, there talked with him two men, which were Moses and Elias; Who appeared in glory, and spake of his decease that he should accomplish at Jerusalem.*

p. 73.

SERMON V.

The Atonement.

Psalm xxii.—1. *" My God! My God!*
" Why hast thou forsaken me?" p. 89.

(Preached on Good-Friday.)

SERMON VI.

The State of the Departed.

Zechariah i.—5. *Your fathers, where are they?* p. 105.

SERMON VII.

The Name of God glorified.

John xii.—28. *" Father, glorify thy name!" Then came there a voice from Heaven, saying, "I have both glorified it, and will glorify it again."* p. 127.

Contents.

SERMON VIII.
The Vanity of Human Wishes.

Job vi.—8, 9. *Oh that I might have my requeſt, and that God would grant me the thing that I long for, Even that it would pleaſe God to deſtroy me!* p. 147.

SERMON IX.
The juſt Judgments of God.

1 Kings xxi.—29. " *Seeſt thou, how Ahab humbleth himſelf before me? Becauſe he humbleth himſelf before me, I will not bring the evil in his days, but in his ſon's days will I bring the evil upon his houſe.*" p. 165.

SERMON X.
The Cloſe of the Year.

Iſaiah lxiv.—6. *We all do fade as a leaf.* p. 187.

SERMON XI.
The Nature of Chriftian Faith.

Hebrews xi.—1. *Now faith is the fub-ftance of things hoped for, the evidence of things not feen.* p. 209.

SERMON XII.
The Object of Chriftian Faith.

John xiv.—1. *" Ye believe in GOD; " believe alfo in me."* p. 229.

SERMON XIII.
The Triumphs of Chriftian Faith.

1 John v.—5. *Who is he that overcometh the world, but he that believeth that Jefus is the fon of God?* p. 253.

SERMON XIV.
The Foundation of Chriftian Hope.

Hebrews xiii.—5. *" I will never leave " thee, nor forfake thee."* p. 275.

SERMON XV.

The Promise of Christian Hope.

Micah ii.—10. *" Arise ye, and depart—*
" for this is not your rest." p. 295.

SERMON XVI.

The Christian's Warfare.

Job i.—6, 7. *Now there was a day, when the sons of God came to present themselves before the Lord, and Satan came also among them.*
And the Lord said unto Satan, " Whence " comest thou?" Then Satan answered the Lord, and said, " FROM GOING TO *"* AND FRO IN THE EARTH, AND FROM *"* WALKING UP AND DOWN IN IT." p. 317.

SERMON XVII.

The Christian's Defence.

Psalm xci. 2. *I will say of the Lord, " He " is my refuge, and my fortress—my " GOD—in Him will I trust."* p. 341.

SERMON XVIII.
The Christian's Joy.

Matthew xiv.—27. "*Be of good cheer;
it is I: be not afraid!*"   p. 365.

SERMON. XIX.
The Christian's Rest.

Psalm iii. 5. *I laid me down and slept: I awaked, for the Lord sustained me.* p. 391.

SERMON XX.
The Christian's Glory.

Hebrews xii.—22, 23, 24. *Ye are come unto Mount Sion, and unto the city of the Living God, the heavenly Jerusalem; and to an innumerable company of angels,*
To the general assembly and Church of the first-born, which are written in Heaven, and to God the Judge of all, and to the spirits of just men made perfect,
And to JESUS, *the Mediator of the new Covenant.*   p. 409.

(Preached on All Saints' Day.)

CORRECTIONS.

P.	14. l. 17, 18. *read*	inveterate
	47. 3.	in the midſt
	54. note 2. l. 2.	defcription
	76. 12.	declarations
	96. 3.	me ?
	102. 12.	many grievous things
	104. 19.	our tongue
	112. 9.	blood ſhedding
	113. 13.	thoſe hours
	169. 13.	explain away
	230. 8.	this day, our Lord
	262. 21.	ſuch an exceeding
	295. 3.	of his adoption
	299. 21.	no peace :
	309. 16.	hand in hand with miſery,

SERMON I.

ON THE CLERICAL CHARACTER.

A VISITATION-SERMON.

(Firſt printed, A. D. 1794.)

SERMON I.

ON THE CLERICAL CHARACTER.

TITUS ii.—7, 8.

In all things shewing thyself a pattern of good works: in doctrine shewing uncorruptness, gravity, sincerity,
Sound speech, that cannot be condemned; that he that is of the contrary part may be ashamed, having no evil thing to say of you.

YOU have in these words a portrait, drawn by the hand of a master, which describes a faithful minister of Christ, a steward of the mysteries of God. By this exemplar he must regulate his life, who would do the office of an Evangelist, who would glorify his Father on earth, and would finish the work given him to perform. There needs no more to convince the Ambaſſadors of Jeſus of the importance, the dignity, the deep reſponſibility of their calling. The inſtructions delivered by the Apoſtle to his adopted ſon are ſo diſtinct, ſo explicit, that they can neither be miſconceived nor miſapprehended. We may neglect—we may contemn—we may diſobey; but when the precept has once founded in our ears, the plea of ignorance is taken away from us for ever.

Without endeavouring, therefore, to diſguiſe or palliate—without attempting to explain away goſpel-truths, out of a falſe and miſtaken delicacy, I ſhall endeavour to ſubmit to this reverend and honoured audience my ideas of the obligations laid upon us, by our engagement in the ſervice of religion—aware, that in the fulleſt ſenſe of the Apoſtle's words, "I
"ſpeak

"speak to them that know the law"—conscious, that I am addressing those, who, in rank, in years, in wisdom, are far my superiors; and, (with somewhat a better apology for my presumption), feeling as he *ought* to have felt, who discoursed on military subjects in the presence of Hannibal.

Notwithstanding these discouragements, the occasion of our assembly calls for reflections of this nature; and the circumstances of the times into which we are thrown, stamp them with a character of more than common solemnity. The events, which the four preceding years have brought forth, as connected with the general interests of Christianity, are too striking, and too momentous, to be silently passed over. When the judgments of God are in the earth, the lesson of righteousness is not merely designed for the sufferers under those judgments. The fall of the backsliding Israel was meant

meant, by a gracious Providence, to be a warning to the treacherous Judah. When the eſtabliſhment of the Church of England is openly and undiſguiſedly attacked by thoſe who have long been attempting its demolition in ſecret, we know not what may enſue; we know not to what trials our Divine CORRECTOR may think it neceſſary to call us. Though it may be urged that our dangers are apparently leſſened, let us not too fondly truſt to the ſpecious calm. Let us not think that it is peace, ſo long as the devices of anti-chriſtian ſedition, and her witchcrafts are ſo many.

The words of my text have a reference to the life, and to the doctrine of the Miniſters of the Goſpel; in both of which they are directed to advance as nearly as poſſible towards perfection, for this eſpecial reaſon, that others of a contrary part may be aſhamed, having no evil thing to to say of persons, whom they are prone to censure, and studious to condemn.

I. The subject, therefore, naturally divides itself into three parts; the first of which we shall dismiss in silence. We shall not detain you a moment by attempting to prove, that the *life* of a preacher of the Gospel should be, as far as the infirmity of human nature will allow, exemplary. On such a topic discussion is useless, and argument superfluous. If there is any truth in religion —if the word of God standeth sure— holiness, which becometh his house and his altar, becometh likewise those who are called on to minister at that altar.

II. With respect to the *doctrines* enjoined us to preach, the words of the holy Apostle seem themselves to point out those particulars necessary to be insisted on. The servant of God is directed in his

his teaching to shew uncorruptness; gravity; sincerity; sound speech, that cannot be condemned. His words must be *uncorrupt*—not basely adapted to the prejudices and propensities of his audience. Whether they will hear, or whether they will forbear, he must speak boldly, as he ought to speak. God hath sent him on a most important errand— to proclaim death as the retribution of sin, and eternal life for them who repent and believe in Christ. Disinterested in his conduct, and far removed from those mean and sordid principles which actuate the hireling, he must be proof against all the temptations of filthy lucre; and must be no more allured by the delusive smile of wickedness, than terrified by its frown. His exhortations must be made with a *gravity* and solemnity suitable to the awfulness of his subject. If he feels the force of the message he is sent to proclaim, he cannot dwell on the wonders of divine mercy, on the

terrors

terrors of divine indignation, with cold and miserable indifference. The fire of zeal and devotion will kindle, and he will speak aright with his tongue. While he repeats the denunciations of God's wrath against sin, while he invites mankind to the privileges afforded them by redeeming love, he must surely be warmed and animated by the light of divine truth. Of all persons he is most engaged to revere that word, which is, as he well knows, the very word of God. That he should therefore speak with *sincerity*, is the necessary consequence of his belief. If he has neither maturely weighed, nor upon conviction embraced in his own person the doctrines of our holy faith, how can he presume to enforce them upon others? How can he attempt to win his hearers by invitations to that mercy—how can he alarm them by threats of that vengeance, which himself neither loves nor fears? Hypocrisy, in all cases a foul and dangerous crime,

crime, is here exhibited in its most odious form. If there be on earth a character more completely detestable than all others—if there be an enormity of guilt which cries to Heaven more especially for punishment, it is that of the minister of the Gospel, who dares to pronounce with his lips those truths against which his heart is revolting; and the infidel who *preaches* Christ, though perhaps not so dangerous to mankind, is personally involved in delinquency of a deeper dye, than the infidel who *blasphemes* him.

The case, in short, stands thus. If we are convinced of the *truth* of our religion, we shall, in our doctrine, shew *sincerity*; if we are persuaded of its *importance*, we shall shew due *gravity*; if we are sensible of the *obligations* it lays on us, we shall shew *uncorruptness*; while all these sentiments, combining their influence on the mind, will cause us to utter on every occasion

occasion *found speech that cannot be condemned.* We shall not shrink from our christian duty, because it is the fashionable attempt of the day to decry the orthodox principles of our faith, and to establish a system of vapid, lifeless, spurious ethics in its stead. The plenary inspiration of those scriptures, by which alone the true God is revealed to mankind—the atonement made for a guilty world—the divine nature of HIM who made that atonement—his incarnation, his life, his miracles, his death, his resurrection, his return to the glory of his Father—the divinity and attributes of the Holy Ghost—the union of the three Persons in one eternal Godhead; a future state of punishment among the spirits of darkness, as well as state of glory among the children of light; the resurrection of the body in the last day; its re-union to the soul; and that happiness, or misery, to which both will be consigned, according to the sentence of a righteous

righteous Judge;—all thefe folemn and momentous truths muft be diligently and earneftly enforced upon mankind, as the only certain bafis of virtue; the only fure foundation on which to reft our hopes of prefent or future welfare. "We "know," faith the beloved Apoftle, "that the Son of God is come, and hath "given us an underftanding, that we "may know him that is true, and we are "in him that is true, even in his fon Je- "fus Chrift. This is the true God, and "eternal life.—Little children, keep "yourfelves from idols!"

On this fubject we may furely be pardoned for dwelling with more than common earneftnefs, fince we have lived to fee the day, when a confiderable part of the once chriftian world has renounced all dependance on a Saviour, and, virtually, on a God. "Reafon" has there its temples, its priefts, and its facrifices— bloody facrifices, and ferocious priefts! "O my foul, come not thou into their "fecret:

" secret: unto their assembly, mine
" honour, be not thou united!"
They shew their new-created faith by
their works; by their fruits do we know
them. When our hearts sicken over recitals of massacre and murder—when we
shudder at the narratives of their ingenious cruelty, and their expeditious
systems of destruction—we cannot but
reverse the famous exclamation of old,
and cry out, with just sentiments of indignation, " Behold, how these infidels
" ABHOR one another!"

III. That there are, even in this
country, busy, restless, malicious adversaries—that they have long been secretly
meditating our destruction, and that, of
late years, they have attempted it in a
more open and decisive manner, is a
truth, which we must be blind indeed
not to acknowledge. The spirit, which
at all times *lurketh* in the children of
disobedience, and which hath ever
moulded

moulded them to his purpose since the first-born Cain shed the blood of an innocent martyr, hath in these latter days walked abroad with a degree of triumphant elevation. Fatally successful elsewhere, his emissaries attempted to give effect to their stratagems here. " They " who have turned the world upside " down, came hither also." Our ecclesiastical and civil establishment was the object of their avowed hostility. Could they but have accomplished the overthrow of either part of our system, they doubted not that the downfall of its associate would speedily follow. Therefore did they encourage themselves in mischief—therefore did they proclaim inveterate war against loyalty and religion, and set up their banners for tokens. Fain would they have planted their " abomination that maketh desolate" amidst the ruins of thrones and altars: that tree, whose fruit is unto profanation, and the end thereof everlasting death: that tree,

tree, which (like the fabled poifon-fhrub of the eaftern world) caufes all other vegetation to languifh and die; which creates a defert around its noxious trunk, and rejoices in horror and devaftation. And were the ftately pines, the glory of Lebanon, and all the trees of the foreft, to be abandoned for *this?* Were they to fall, proftrate and overthrown, before it? Above the reft, was this SACRED OAK, which for fo long a period has braved the violence of winds and ftorms, was this to be rooted up, though the hills are covered with the fhadow of it, and the boughs thereof are like the goodly cedars?

Such, however, was the mifchief we had to apprehend, though they who beft knew the extent of it affect to fpeak moft contemptuoufly of our apprehenfions. Even now would the meditated evil take place, did not Divine Providence watch over us for good, and, by awakening us to a fenfe of our danger, difappoint the purpofe of our affailants.

What means of refiftance are afforded to the minifters of Chrift, in circumftances like thefe? How are we, againft whom the fhafts are levelled with peculiar animofity, how are we to repel affaults of fo threatening a nature? Certainly not by employing malice and revenge on our part, in oppofition to the enemies of our order. The weapons of our warfare are fpiritual, and only fpiritual. The fervant of God muft not ftrive. If he contend for the faith, it muft be with the *fhield* of faith, and with the fword of the fpirit, which is the word of God. To the rage of his adverfaries, he muft oppofe meeknefs; to their calumnies, innocence; to their open perfecution, long-fuffering; to their treacherous machinations, the noble fimplicity of truth and virtue.

Thefe

'These are our best resources; woe unto us, if we are so negligent, or so unprincipled, as not to avail ourselves of them! If the preacher of the gospel considers himself as one sent, not to feed, but to devour the flock—if he considers his profession in no higher light than as the means of supplying his necessities, or administering to his pleasures—if he counts the duties of his office a toilsome drudgery, a tax laid upon his emoluments, a task of mere lip-labour, and discharges these duties accordingly—if nothing but his habit, and scarcely that, distinguishes his sacerdotal character—if in his life and conversation, his manners, his recreations, his language, he studiously imitates the conduct of the more gay and dissipated part of mankind—if in his doctrine, regardless what is truth, or whether there be any truth at all, he deals out the frigid morality he cares not to practise, and totally shuns to declare the counsel of God—if, while the enemies are at the very gate of the city, breathing war and defiance, the fortress should be thus wickedly and basely deserted—what marvel, if they should be permitted to sweep our ecclesiastical establishment with the besom of destruction*? What marvel, if they should root up, and devour, and triumph, and blaspheme? What marvel, if malice, or perverseness, or indiscriminating ignorance, should unjustly confound our cause with its advocates, and should take occasion to revile the faith once delivered to the Saints—that faith, which was enforced and proclaimed by their doctrines, illustrated and adorned by their lives, sealed and witnessed by their blood? If this were in general the case, then indeed the mischief would be incalculable, and the overflowing flood would carry all before it.

But, beloved, we are persuaded better things of the order concerning which we

* Isaiah xiv. 23.

speak.

speak. Though there may be lamentable instances of guilt and corruption among those who have dedicated themselves to the ministry (as was the case in its earliest days, when the Apostles themselves had a traitor among their number), we cannot but indulge the well-grounded hope, that an almost infinite majority of the clergy are faithful and diligent servants of their blessed Master—that zeal, learning, piety, and those graces which best become the christian character, do flourish and abound among them—that they exhibit a pattern of good works in their lives—that they are uncorrupt, grave, sincere, and orthodox, in their doctrine. By these, under the patronage of a Sovereign whom the Church of England glories in acknowledging as its Head, and with the co-operation of many illustrious characters among the laity, the torrent of infidelity, vice, and licentiousness, which would have deluged our country, has hitherto been not un-

unsuccessfully stemmed—the poisoned darts of the enemy have fallen, harmless and ineffectual to the ground—the storm has been averted, which loured around us, and which fell in all its fury upon others.

We have seen the rage of the oppressor let loose upon mankind—we have seen the judgment beginning at the house of God. At the commencement of those events which now astonish the world, it was the privilege of one luminous mind to trace the infant monster to its horrible maturity. During the progress, and in the consummation of those events, we have all obtained conviction. If here the arm of the destroying angel has been arrested—if here the temple, the altar, and the ministers of God are rescued from profanation, let us not be lulled into morbid and lethargic repose—still less let us ascribe to *merit*, what is due only to *mercy*. Alas! were the faithful

-ful paſtors, who have fallen under the daggers of aſſaſſination, ſinners above all the ſervants of Chriſt? Far otherwiſe. As gold in the furnace have they been tried, and received as a burnt-offering. However we may differ from them on ſome important doctrinal points, we muſt be loſt to a ſenſe of all that is great and glorious, if we do not applaud their heroic conſtancy, their unconquerable zeal, and that hope, full of immortality, which ſurmounted the fear of diſſolution. Faithful confeſſors, intrepid martyrs, they rejoiced in following the ſteps of their Redeemer—and their Church, ſolitary, and a widow, is more venerable, more lovely amidſt its tears, than in all the pride and pageantry of bridal magnificence.

With ſuch a ſpectacle as this preſented before our eyes, how can we refuſe to take warning? How can we but pray, that

that if God should think it necessary to punish, he would correct us in mercy, and would not stir up the utmost fierceness of his wrath? Avert the stroke, my brethren, as far as your own exertions can avert it. Awake to righteousness and sin not; let your conversation be as becometh the Gospel of Christ; let your light shine before men. Let the ministers of truth, established to turn the disobedient to the wisdom of the just, exemplify by their lives the excellence of that faith, which at all times, and particularly in times like the present, demands their unshaken allegiance. Let them take heed to themselves and to their doctrine, for conscience' sake, and with a view to the glory of God; not merely because they are exposed to the scrutinizing eye of malevolence. Let them, in the spirit and power of Elias, repair the altar of JEHOVAH, where it is broken down *. Let them preserve, with faith-

* See 1 Kings xviii, 30.

ful affiduity, every fpark of celeftial fire that can be found among thofe hallowed embers, which their zeal, affifted by the Spirit of God, may fan into a flame of true and primitive piety. Thus much is not only in their power, but a part of their bounden duty. For the reft, " It is the Lord, let him do what " feemeth him good." If at laft the blow fhould fall upon us—if we fhould be conftrained to fuffer, as our fellow-fervants and fellow-labourers have fuffered, then let us remember, that the trial of our faith worketh patience; that greater is He who is for us, than they who are againft us; that bleffed are we, when we are perfecuted for righteoufnefs' fake, for our reward is great in Heaven. Let us confider Him who endured fuch contradictions of finners againft himfelf, left we be wearied and faint in our minds. Through the Captain of our falvation, though we are even called upon to refift unto blood, we cannot but be finally vic-

victorious. From the height of that Heaven, to which he was exalted after his fufferings, he beholds his faithful fervants ftruggling in this world of forrows againft the power and malice of their enemies. He beholds them, with fuch fentiments as actuate a father, when he fends a beloved fon into the field of battle, to affert the honour of his country. He beholds them, as once he faw his chofen Apoftles, driven by the winds, and toffed by the tempeft. And till He, whofe omnipotence can rule the rage of the fea, the noife of its waves, and the madnefs of the people, till He fhall in his own good time fay unto thefe furious affailants, "Peace, be ftill,"let us hear him addreffing his militant Church from the habitation of his holinefs and of his glory; "Why are ye fearful, O ye of little "faith? Behold, I am with you always, "even unto the end of the world. "Amen."

SERMON II.

THE CREATION.

SERMON II.

THE CREATION.

GENESIS i.—1.

In the beginning God created the Heaven and the earth.

THE Power, Wisdom, and Goodness of God, as displayed in the formation of the world, present such an assemblage of wonders to the eye of faith, that if the mind of man, fixed on this one vast contemplation, should without intermission medi-

meditate thereon, the limits of our existence would be insufficient for us to comprehend, in their full perfection, the marvellous works of the Almighty. To such a subject the Christian might direct his thoughts with new delight, and new instruction, and new astonishment, till the angel of death awakened him from his musings, and summoned him to behold the face of God.

And if the work of Creation displays such a boundless and inexhaustible treasure of divine knowledge, what shall we say, when the Maker of the world, and of all things it contains, exhibits himself to our view as its Redeemer, its Restorer from ruin, the Author of new and spiritual life, that life, which is the Light of men, and which flows from the same celestial source? " In the beginning was " the WORD, and the Word was with " God, and the Word was GOD. All
" things

"things were made by him, and without him was not any thing made, that was made."

In the following difcourfe I fhall endeavour to fet before you the natural hiftory of the world—perfect in its creation—thrown into confufion by fin—renewed by the divine mercy in Chrift—and now waiting the laft awful doom, when the fame God who created the elements around us, fhall, by his Almighty word, deftroy them—when the heavens and earth fhall perifh, and "time fhall be no more."

Confiderations more awful and interefting than thefe cannot be prefented to the mind. They arreft the attention with pre-eminent force—They awaken terror, and they lead to extafy. The fubject is fo great, fo fublime, fo myfterious, that it tranfcends all human ability to do it juftice. It is the theme of of Angels: and it has been their theme since the commencement of the world— since the day, when " the morning " ſtars firſt ſang together, and all the " ſons of God ſhouted for joy." Proſtrate before the eternal throne, they worſhip Him that liveth for ever and ever, and caſt their crowns before the throne, ſaying, " Thou art worthy, O " Lord, to receive glory and honour, " and power, *for thou haſt created all things*; " and for thy pleaſure they are, and were " created."

We are aware that the daring voice of infidelity has preſumed even to call in queſtion the faƈt recorded in my text, and to ſubſtitute impious and atheiſtical theories in its room. May that power, which turneth the heart as the rivers of water, grant to theſe unhappy ſelf-deceivers the grace of converſion! *We* glory in our Chriſtian profeſſion; and we believe the word of God. We believe, and therefore do we speak. "I have not "written unto you," saith St. John to his disciples, "because ye know not the "truth, *but because ye know it.*" And St. Peter: "I will not be negligent to "put you always in remembrance of "these things, *though ye know them*, and "be established in the present truth." If there be any here so unhappy, as not to be stedfast in the faith once delivered to the saints, let him lift up his eyes to the heavens, and look on the earth beneath. Heaven and earth are full of the Majesty of the divine glory. Under the guidance of the word of God, by considering the work he will acknowledge the Work-master, and will worship the Father everlasting.

We say, "under the guidance of the "word of God," because we know no other way, by which understanding is given to man. Nor do we consider this as the debasement, but, on the contrary, ry, as the higheſt exaltation of human reaſon. The inviſible things of him are from the creation of the world clearly ſeen—and why? *becauſe God hath ſhewed them.* In this conſiſts the real dignity of our nature, that its powers are called forth, not by any intrinſic ability or reſources of its own, but by the all-powerful inſpiration of the Holy Spirit, and the grace of God, ever preſent with the oracles of truth. The Apoſtle is expreſs and deciſive upon this ſubject. "Through faith (which, as he elſewhere ſays, cometh by *hearing*) THROUGH FAITH we underſtand, that the worlds were framed by the Word of God." It is Revelation which gives us the opportunity of knowing the Creator of the univerſe, as he would manifeſt himſelf to mankind. Illuminated by his divine aid, the fire kindles, and darkneſs is turned into light. Then, in the various appearances of the heavens, in the orbs of the ſun and moon, in meteors, planets, conſtellations,

lations, in comets and eclipses, in the showers and dew, ice cast out like morsels, clouds brought from the ends of the earth, lightnings and thunder, winds drawn from the divine treasuries, and storms which fulfil the word of GOD—in all these we contemplate the marvellous works of the Most High, himself greater than all, and unsearchable. We adore Him, who hath revealed to us a portion of his ways, and hath enabled us to know " how the earth was made, and the " operations of the elements, the begin-" ning, ending, and midst of the times, " the alterations of the turning [of the " world*] and the change of seasons, the " circuits of years, and the positions of " stars—' who hath not only given us visual powers to behold the beauty of these gems of heaven, but intellectual

* Τροπῶν ἀλλαγάς. Wisd. vii. 18. The translators have substituted the words [of the sun] to supply the ellipsis.

SERM. II.

ability to difcover their periodical revolutions—to calculate, with the moſt accurate precifion, the times of their appearance, and to afcertain the exact moment, when for a while their light fhall be withdrawn. Thus is true philofophy the handmaid of true religion: and to a mind unprejudiced by the oppofitions of fcience falfely fo called, the heavens declare the glory of GOD, and the firmament fheweth his handywork.

If we turn our eyes to the earth, we behold a treafury of equal wonders. But here our knowledge is comparatively defective. Notwithſtanding all the arts, and all the induſtry, and all the curiofity, and all the avarice of man, we are ſtill very ignorant of the nature and properties of that aftonifhing planet on which the Almighty has placed us*. Here

*. The diameter of the earth is ſtated to be at the equator 7940 miles; at the poles 7903. See Whitehurſt's Account of the French experiments made by order of Louis XV.

theory

theory muft be uncertain, and experiment inconclufive. The only glimmerings of light afforded us are thofe which the Mofaic hiftory incidentally imparts; and with thefe the refult of every inveftigation fairly made, to the extent of human powers, has been found exactly to coincide*. Thence we gather, that when the Almighty Agent firft called the world into being, it was, during the affemblage of its component parts, in fhapelefs confufion, or as it is otherwife called, *chaos*—that the blended elements, themfelves in a ftate of fluidity, were covered by water, and that darknefs was upon the face of the deep. Then did the SPIRIT OF GOD †, moving on the face of the waters, call thefe wild and jarring atoms into order, and harmony, and beauty. Then did the WORD OF GOD †, by whom all things were made, give his mandate, *and there was light*. By vir-

---

* See M. De Luc's Geological Letters.

Compare Pfal. xxxiii. 6.

tue of this emanation from above, similar particles began to unite one with another—water with water—earth with earth—air with air*. On the second day, the expansive firmament of heaven † was fixed over the earth—on the third, the dry land appeared, and the ocean retired to its appropriate limits. Light and heat now gradually increasing, and being concentrated by the divine command in the great luminary of heaven, the sun appeared in the firmament, a marvellous instrument, the work of the Most High, and shone with its full lustre on the newly-created world. The solar and planetary system received unerring laws; upon earth the beauties of vegetation took place; the terrestrial globe, the mighty waters, were peopled with their respective inhabitants; man, the vicegerent of GOD, was made in his image, taught by his inspiration, and

---

* See Whitehurst's Theory of the Earth.

† Called by Plato Τάσις. See Parkhurst's Hebrew Lexicon, in v. רקע.

by

by divine right invested in his Paradise with universal dominion. The world and its elements, nature animated and inanimate, were at peace. GOD saw every thing that he had made, and, behold, it was very good.

Prepare now for a different recital. Mark how sin at first deformed, and afterwards for a while destroyed this fair creation. Turn your eyes to offending man, banished from the favour and presence of GOD, an exile from the delights of Eden. See death, and enmity, and desolation, introduced into the world. Pursue the melancholy enquiry, till the moment, when increasing enormities on the part of man provoked the long-threatened, long-delayed, vengeance of heaven. What alterations do we behold in the frame of nature! Lo, " the foun-" tains of the great deep are broken up;" the internal abyss of waters, (rarified and dilated by the central fire) with a shock

shock most tremendous, with an explosion* beyond all idea, bursts the terrestrial globe into innumerable fragments. Waving all minute discussion, allow me to remark, that by the power of these most mighty agents in nature, let loose by divine justice upon mankind, the bottom of the antediluvian sea was elevated, and the former world, with all its inhabitants (save those miraculously preserved in the ark) was plunged beneath the waters. A thousand proofs of this might be adduced, had we leisure to pursue the subject with more minute investigation. Every circumstance tends to demonstrate, that we behold and inhabit the ruin of a dismembered fabric †. The craggy rock, the cavern, the precipice, quarries, mines, volcanos, fossils, marine animals entombed in the solid substance of stones and marbles in

---

* The expansive power of *steam* is to that of *gunpowder* nearly as 14000 to 500, or 28 to 1. *Whitehurst.*

† ἀρχαίω κόσμω ἐκ ἰδύσαιο. 2 Pet. ii. 5.

all

all parts of the world, or found in abundance on the tops of mountains at immenfe diftances from the fea, bear witnefs to this wreck of nature. Even the pebble under our feet, rounded by external force, or fhattered by violent collifion—even the meaneft grain of fand has a voice, to put infidelity to filence, and difprove the impious affertion, " that all things continue as they were " from the beginning of the creation." The unbeliever on this fubject purpofely fhuts his eyes againft conviction. He cannot endure the alarming truth, that God, who once chaftifed the whole world for fin, will for fin hereafter yet more fearfully punifh it in his anger. " Of " this," as the Apoftle argues, " they " are *willingly ignorant*"—they feel a dreadful intereft in concealing from themfelves, " that by the word of God " the heavens were of old, and the earth, " ftanding out of the water and in the " water." They hear not that almighty voice,

voice, speaking in vengeance, "where-by," at whose command, "the world that then was, being overflowed with water, perished." They tremble to think, and strive to evade the thought, "that the heavens and earth which are "now, are by the same word kept in "store, reserved unto fire against the "day of judgement, and perdition of "ungodly men." We, my brethren, have ourselves seen the day, when Atheism was authoritatively proclaimed by those who trampled on the ruins of a christian throne, and offerings were paid to the idol, Reason, on altars once dedicated to Christ. But it was a system too monstrous, too horrid, to take root even in the polluted soil to which it was consigned. The storm, which for a while shook the earth, passed away with the dæmons who excited it. They are gone, and their place knoweth them no more.

But

The Creation.

SERM. II.

But we pursue these subjects no further. Other contemplations, more immediately connected with ourselves, of still nearer import, as the concerns of the soul must be more momentous than those of the body, are presented to our minds. With the denunciation of temporal death, came the precious promise of eternal life. Fallen man was commanded to lift up his head, and rejoice in heavenly mercy. The world, degenerate and debased, was nevertheless visited by the REDEEMER, and all the ends of the earth beheld the salvation of God. Such are the benefits which faith and hope exhibit to us in the great mystery of godliness; such is the efficacy of that precious blood, of that one perfect oblation. When the soul of man was in a state of gloom and confusion, far more terrible than the primæval chaos of nature, the voice of God was heard, speaking in righteousness, mighty to save. "Let there be light! "Let there be liberty! Let there be sal- "vation!

"vation! Deliver them from going down "to the pit—I have found a ranfom." In this view the bleffed and holy Apoftle compares the wonders of redemption with thofe of the creation. God, he fays, who commanded the light to fhine out of darknefs, hath fhined in our hearts, to give the " light of the know- " lege of the glory of God, in the face " of Jefus Chrift." A feparation is thus again made between light and darknefs; between the promife of eternal life given to faith and repentance, and the juft fentence of death everlafting, the accurfed wages of fin. Man, formed originally in the image of the Almighty, is raifed from the dejection into which difobedience had thrown him, and is exalted " unto the meafure of the ftature of the " fulnefs of Chrift." Chrift is in him the hope of glory; and (if he does not fruftrate the work of grace) in fpite of all the malice of hell, he fhall hereafter be permitted to eat of the fruit of the

Tree

Tree of Life, which is in the midst of the Paradise of God.

Take heed then, my beloved brethren, that ye forfeit not these exceeding great and glorious privileges; adhere to them, as to an anchor of the soul, sure and stedfast. How shall ye escape, if ye neglect so great salvation? O do not lose your interest in a Redeemer's merits—do not render the blood of Christ of none effect to your souls! Flee from sin, as from the face of a serpent—give all diligence to repel its pestilential assaults. Let zeal and devotion, let faith and love, guard your hearts against the approach of evil, as studiously, as successfully, as the Cherubim with their flaming swords kept the garden of Eden from the intrusion of guilt. Take fast hold of instruction; let it not go; keep it, for it is your life.

For

SERM. II.

For lo, our God will come, and will not keep filence. There fhall go before him a confuming fire, and a mighty tempeft fhall be ftirred up round about him. He fhall call the heavens from above, and the earth, that he may judge his people. The all-powerful voice which produced the univerfe, fhall annihilate it. I would fain engage your folemn attention; I would fain fet before you the terrors of the Lord: but no thoughts, no words can pourtray them. Language cannot exprefs the convulfive ftruggles of an expiring world. Imagination cannot conceive the awful majefty of His prefence, before whom the heavens and earth fhall flee away, and have no place—before whom the orbs of light fhall vanifh—the moon fhall be confounded, and the fun afhamed. Human nature fhrinks from the idea of that found, which fhall difturb the fleep of death, and burft the receffes of the grave: at which " the earth fhall be
" utterly

" utterly broken down—the earth shall
" be clean dissolved—the earth shall be
" moved exceedingly—the earth shall
" reel to and fro like a drunkard, and
" shall be removed like a cottage; while
" the transgression thereof shall be heavy
" upon it, and it shall fall, and not rise
" again."

Then, O then, "turn you to the strong
" hold, ye prisoners of hope!" Behold
the Captain of your salvation coming to
deliver you. Behold him, bearing in his
hand the sacred banner of redemption.
See him exhibit on it the sentence of
death, cancelled, annulled, expiated by
his all-sufficient blood. Though the
day of the Lord is great and very terrible, and none can abide it, hear his
gracious voice, proclaiming in accents
of love: " Look unto me, and be ye
" saved—for mercy rejoiceth against
" judgement." Thus, when dead in our
sins, shall we be quickened together with
him:

him: for he will forgive us all trespasses on our sincere repentance, "blotting out the hand-writing of ordinances that was against us, which was contrary to us, and taking it out of the way, nailing it to his cross." The heavens shall vanish away like smoke, and the earth shall wax old as a garment, and they that dwell therein shall die in like manner: but his salvation shall be for ever, and his righteousness shall not be abolished.

Heaven and earth shall pass away, but his word shall not pass away: they shall perish, but his promise remaineth. Hear that promise, and depart in peace.

"Behold, I create new heavens, and a new earth, saith the Lord, and the former shall not be remembered, nor come into mind. And there shall be no more curse; but the throne of God and of the Lamb shall be therein, and his fervants fhall ferve him, and they fhall reign for ever and ever. He which is in the midſt of the throne fhall feed them, and fhall lead them unto living fountains of waters, and the Lord God fhall wipe away all tears from their eyes. The fun fhall be no more their light by day, neither for brightnefs fhall the moon give light unto them : but the Lord fhall be unto them an everlaſting light, and their God, their glory."

To whom, Father, Son, and Holy Ghoſt, our great Creator, Redeemer, and Comforter, be afcribed, as is moſt due, all honour, power, might, majeſty, and dominion, for ever and ever. Amen.

SERMON

SERMON III.

THE UNITY OF GOD.

PREACHED ON TRINITY-SUNDAY.

E

SERMON III.

THE UNITY OF GOD.

MARK x.—18.

*And Jesus said unto him, " Why callest thou
" me good? There is none good but One:
" that is, GOD."*

THERE is not, perhaps, a passage in
the sacred writings, whereon the pride
of heresy and infidelity dwells with more
peculiar delight, than on the words of
our blessed Saviour which I have selected
for our meditation this day: and which
I have selected, without the smallest apprehension

prehenfion of their conveying, when fairly and deliberately examined, the interpretation which prejudice and fcepticifm is prone to affign to them.

During our Lord's abode on earth, it was the favourite employment of his enemies, to feek his overthrow by means of fome expreffion from his own lips, which might be irreconcileable with the ftrictnefs of their own eftablifhed fyftem of religion. They frequently queftioned him, and urged him to fpeak on many things; " laying wait for him, and endeavouring to catch fomething out of his mouth, that they might accufe him." The Pharifees brought him a notorious delinquent, in hopes that if he condemned, or acquitted, he might be found either to ufurp a power not his own, or to contradict the law of Mofes. The Sadducees (a fet of infidels, who, being prevented by no falutary reftrictions, had infinuated themfelves into the

facred

sacred office of the priesthood), though they denied the resurrection from the dead, affected to seek information on the subject as if they had actually believed, while in fact they were wilfully attempting to create and not to remove difficulties, on a topic so sublime and mysterious. "*In the resurrection, when* "*they rise*, how shall this be?" The Lawyers, that is, the teachers or doctors of the Mosaic law, to whom the people looked for guidance and information in all causes of doubt and perplexity, demand of him, with a sarcastic affectation of ignorance, "which is the great com-
"mandment of the law?" Woe unto you, Pharisees, Sadducees, Lawyers, hypocrites, how wretchedly were those privileges cast away, or rather how basely were they abused, which a God of mercy freely offered to his peculiar people! How justly spake the Evangelist of the Redeemer of mankind, "He "came

"came unto his own, and his own received him not*!"

It does not pofitively appear, that the perfon to whom our Saviour addreffed the words of my text, was an emiffary of thefe infidious opponents. On the contrary, his faith feems to have been fincere, as far as it extended; but weak and imperfect in the extreme. Impreffed with a fenfe, that fome exertion on his part was neceffary to obtain the rewards of the bleffed, in that future ftate of exiftence which he firmly believed, he fought information from Chrift on this fubject with the impaffioned eagernefs of hafte, with humble teftimonies of reverence. He came *running* †, and *kneeled*

---

* There is no poffibility of rendering this paffage in conformity to the Greek, but by a paraphrafe. Chrift came εἰς τὰ ἴδια, to the *things* which properly belonged to him—and οἱ ἴδιοι, his own *people*, received him not.

† We have here a remarkable inftance of the *manner of defcription* adopted by St. Mark, which as the acute and ingenious Dr. Townfen obferves, could only be that of one who himfelf had witneffed what he defcribed.

down

down to Jesus, and said, "*Good Master,*
"*what shall I do to inherit eternal life?*
" Thy words have brought conviction
" to my soul. I cannot refuse my as-
" sent to the truths thou hast revealed;
" and I am anxiously desirous to obtain
" a part in the glories which thou hast
" promised to those who believe on thee.
" Teach me, O Lord, the way of thy
" statutes, and I shall keep it unto the
" end."

Alas, how lamentable is it, that so promising a dawn of faith should be so early and so fatally overclouded! The airy edifice waited not for the actual approach of the storm; it shivered to atoms, at the very apprehension of difficulty, danger, and self-denial. No sooner does our Lord make experiment of the constancy of his once eager proselyte, than he departs with a sigh, regretting that he cannot better reconcile present enjoyment with expectations of future

future happiness, but determined at all events to abide by the present, and to risk the future. Our blessed Lord points out the way to escape: the lukewarm, spiritless disciple (if he deserves the name) turns back, with fond attachment, to the world.

It was impossible to avoid stating these few particulars, as connected with the words of my text, and as conveying a very useful, though an alarming lesson: " What shall it profit a man, if he shall " gain the whole world, and lose his " own soul? or what shall a man give " in exchange for his soul? How hardly " shall they that trust in riches, enter " into the kingdom of God?"

But in recommending the assertion of our blessed Saviour to your attention *this day*, I have a still more important and more exalted object in view, which I shall now endeavour to explain, with
the

the divine bleffing, to the fatisfaction of my hearers.

"There is none good but one—that is, God." The propofition is ftated with a force which nothing can refift, and with a precifion which nothing can evade. Unlefs therefore, in our creeds and confeffions of faith, we adhere to this fixed principle fo laid down, we certainly cannot be faid to build on the foundation of that facred legiflator who uttered the memorable words before us.

The Church of England, eftablifhed on the moft fure bafis of Chriftianity, is, in conformity to the letter and fpirit of her bleffed Mafter's doctrine, ftrictly UNITARIAN. Let not my beloved brethren be ftartled at the word. Let them not fhrink from a title, which is the glory of the true believer, becaufe it has been profaned and contaminated by the enemies of our holy faith: becaufe innovating

SERM. III.

ing heretics have dared to ſtigmatize us with idolatry, and to challenge for themſelves, by a bold uſurpation, the name of *Unitarians*, as if we had gods many, and lords many, while in fact we have but " one God, and his name ONE;" his holy, reverend, incommunicable name.

The firſt and leading article of our religion, (while in its cloſe it inveſtigates, as nearly as may be permitted to mortals, the myſterious nature of the divine eſſence) at its commencement declares, with all the dignity of language which becomes the awful ſubject, " There is but ONE living and true " GOD, Everlaſting, without body, " parts, or paſſions—of infinite power, " wiſdom, and goodneſs—the Maker " and preſerver of all things both viſible " and inviſible. And in this UNITY of " Godhead there be THREE PERSONS, of " one ſubſtance, power, and eternity—
" the

"the FATHER, the SON, and the HOLY
"GHOST."

Can any charge then be more grofsly unfounded, can any affertion be more falfe or unprincipled, than that which accufes the orthodox believers of multiplying the objects of religious adoration, and doing homage to more gods than one? On this facred day, whereon the foul ventures to approach to the threfhold of the very Holy of Holies—on which, with an eagle's eye, it prefumes to behold the great and almoft intolerable fplendour of the Lord God Omnipotent, the Church of which we are members adores Him who hath given his fervants grace, not only " to ac-
" knowledge the glory of the eternal
" Trinity, but in the power of the di-
" vine Majefty to worfhip the *Unity:*"
and implores him to keep his fervants ftedfaft in *this* true and incorruptible faith, once delivered to the faints.

That

SERM. III. That our Lord Jesus Christ, the second person in the ONE Godhead, the everlasting Son * of the everlasting Father, did for us men and for our Salvation come down from Heaven—that, in a manner we are utterly unable to comprehend (while we gratefully acknowledge the reality of the fact) the divine nature took human nature on itself, so that the Godhead and manhood were perfectly joined together in one person, never to be divided in one Christ, our Mediator and Redeemer, who died for our sins, and who rose again for our justification—that the Holy Ghost, proceeding from the Father and Son, ONE very and eternal God, of one substance, majesty, and glory in the essence of Jehovah, did by his holy inspiration crown the blessed work—and that these various influences of ONE divine mercy preserved

---

* For a most satisfactory interpretation of this title of the Messiah, the reader is referred to the " Ὁ ἀληθινος," of the late excellent and pious Mr. Hawtrey.

The Unity of God.

us from eternal death, and made us capable of the glories of Heaven—all this we stedfastly believe. But it is so far from militating against the Unity of God, that while we adore the blessed and glorious Trinity, we disclaim, and from our hearts disavow any plurality of worship. We bow down, in humble adoration, before the One Great and glorious name, saying, " Holy, Holy, Holy Lord God Almighty; which art, and wast, and art to come—thou art the God, even thou *alone*—worthy to receive honour, and power, and adoration, and praise—"thou
" art God, and there is none else—thou
" art the Lord, and there is none beside
" thee!"

When we see therefore the Saviour of the world directing his inquisitive proselyte to the grand object of religious adoration (the ONE GOD), we are far from considering these momentous truths as weakened, on which we entirely rely as the sure and certain foundation of Christi-

SERM. III.

Chriftianity. The very man Chrift Jefus, fpeaking in his character as man, afferts that there is none *good*—that there is none abfolutely perfect—none All-wife, All-powerful, All-glorious, but JEHOVAH: the Divine Effence, whereof he partook as fully, as of the human nature which he affumed. Thus the bleffed Jefus is " God of God, Light of Light, very God of very God," who for us men and for our falvation came down from Heaven, and was made man. As man, he difclaims that homage, which it is meet, right, and our bounden duty, to pay to him as God. In his human capacity he fays, " *My Father is greater than* " *I.*" The glory of him that fitteth on the throne is fuperior to that of the only begotten Son of the Father, while in his embaffy of love and mercy to fallen mankind.

" Ye feek to kill me," faith he to the barbarous Jews, " a *man* who hath " told you the truth which I re-
" ceived

"ceived from God." Here again we are diftinctly to feparate the two offices of the Mediator; and to confider him as addreffing his perfecutors in the character of one cloathed with mortality, and fubject to that death which they thirfted to inflict on him—a fituation, inferior indeed to that of the "King Eternal, "Immortal, Invifible, the only wife God:" to whom (neverthelefs) when his work of mercy was over, he thought it no robbery to be equal, being the brightnefs of his glory, the exprefs image of his perfon.

Still more ftriking and appofite are thofe very remarkable words which conclude our Lord's folemn and awful prediction of the day of judgment. "Of that day and hour knoweth no "man—not even the Angels of Hea- "ven—NOR THE SON—but the Fa- "ther!" If there is any force in language—if words have their determinate meaning, an evident inferiority is here implied, indeed expreffed. Nor let

let the adversary and the enemy triumph over us for the avowal. "There is one "God—and one mediator between God "and man, the man Chrift Jefus." Either part of the propofition is abfolutely, is *equally* neceffary—equally effential to the faith we profefs, and to the hope which we cherifh as a ftedfaft anchor of the foul.

One more inftance, and one only, fhall be adduced to prove the *human* nature of Chrift. I felect it from the interefting narrative given us by the Evangelift, with moft affecting fimplicity, of the death, and the revival of Lazarus. When our blefled Saviour approached the place where the remains of his beloved difciple were depofited—when he was about to exhibit an amazing miracle in the prefence of a mixed multitude of friends and enemies, he lifted up his eyes to Heaven in awful preparation, and faid, "Father, I thank thee "that

" that thou haſt heard me—and I knew
" that thou heareſt me always; but be-
" cauſe of the people which ſtand by I
" ſaid it, that they may believe that
" thou haſt ſent me." Here Chriſt, as a
Son, addreſſes Jehovah as a Father; he
repreſents himſelf as one that had offered
up his petitions to Heaven, and had been
heard.

But while, in theſe and a variety of
other inſtances which might be ſet before you, the Saviour ſpeaks of himſelf
as man, we are at the ſame time able
to produce the moſt poſitive and irre-
ſiſtible evidence, that, during his abode on
earth, he as frequently, as clearly, as
unambiguouſly ſpoke of himſelf as God.
It would be a treſpaſs on your patience
to bring forward all the paſſages of ſcripture to which I allude. Yet ſome of
them I may be permitted to point out,
though they are, I truſt, familiar to
your ears—though they are, I humbly
hope,

hope, written on your hearts. You cannot but know on whom ye have believed. You have, doubtlefs, fo learned Chrift, as to be able to give to every man that afketh you, a reafon of the hope that is in you.

Thus then the incarnate God, (with reference not to his human but to his divine nature) beareth witnefs of himfelf—

" I and the Father are ONE *. Before
" Abraham was, I AM. He that hath
" feen me, hath feen the Father. Be-
" lieve me, that I am in the Father, and
" the Father in me. All things that
" the Father hath, are mine. Holy Fa-
" ther, keep through thine own name
" thofe whom thou haft given me, that
" they may be one, as we are."

---

* 'Εγὼ ϰ̀ ὁ Πατὴρ ἓν ἐσμιν. *Unum*: one *fubftance*, differing in perfon.

Hear

Hear alfo what Saint Paul faith—

"Without controverfy great is the myftery of Godlinefs: God was manifefted in the flefh."

Hear alfo what Saint John faith—

"In the beginning was the Word; and the Word was with God; and the Word was God: and the Word was made manifeft, and dwelt among us."

We reft our evidence here; and with it, all our future profpects, all our hopes of endlefs felicity. If we are herein found falfe witneffes of God, our preaching is vain, and your faith is alfo vain. But, as God is true, this our record of his bleffed Son is alfo true.

As the reafonable foul and flefh is one man, fo God and man is one Chrift. Neither his divinity without his humanity,

nity, nor his humanity without his divinity, could have conftituted the true Meffiah, GOD man, the Mediator of the gofpel of grace and pardon, the Angel of the covenant of peace, the Fountain of our everlafting hope, the great Interceffor, able to reconcile all things to himfelf, whether they be things on earth, or things in heaven.

Be aware of this; and when heretics cavil, and infidels blafpheme, be "valiant for the faith." Now the right faith is, that we believe and confefs, that our Lord Jefus Chrift, the Son of God, is God and man. Witnefs this good confeffion before many witneffes. Acknowledge to its full extent the fact announced in my text, that none is good but One, that is God. But reject with abhorrence the peftilent infinuation, that the Author of our falvation, though inferior to the Father as touching his manhood, was not equal to him with respect to his Godhead. As man, our Saviour referred his disciple to JEHOVAH as the BEING in whom all goodness, all glory, all perfection centers, and from whom it flows. As God, he is himself, together with the Father and the Holy Spirit, that Being; the object of all religious adoration. And as with the heart man believeth unto righteousness, and with the mouth confession is made unto salvation, even so believe with your hearts, and confess with your mouths, " that the Godhead " of the Father, of the Son, and of the " Holy Ghost, is all ONE—the glory " equal—the majesty co-eternal."

To whom, as is most due, be ascribed, all honour, praise, and dominion, world without end. Amen.

SERMON IV.

THE TRANSFIGURATION.

SERMON IV.

THE TRANSFIGURATION.

LUKE ix.—29, 30, 31.

And as he prayed, the fashion of his countenance was altered; and his raiment was white and glistering.
And behold, there talked with him two men, which were Moses and Elias;
Who appeared in glory, and spake of his decease that he should accomplish at Jerusalem.

THE stupendous event recorded in my text, and its attendant circumstances, cannot fail to inspire the devout soul with solemn meditations, and to set before

fore the eye of faith a portion of that glory which shall hereafter be more fully revealed. The subject stands nearly connected with things too sublime and awful for human investigation: yet we trust, that information, delight, and comfort may be obtained by considerations on the transfiguration of Christ; and that we may approach the brightness of his presence, without treading too presumptuously on holy ground.

That our blessed Saviour came into the world, not to triumph, but to suffer—that he was meek and lowly, in heart, in manners, in demeanour—that he rejected all adventitious pomp and grandeur, as inconsistent with the spiritual nature of his kingdom, what man can doubt, who reads the history of his humble life? But, as he was not only the despised Son of Mary, but the eternal and ever-blessed Son of God—as he who came in the form of a servant, was

the

the Omnipotent Monarch of Heaven, King of Kings, and Lord of Lords—as he who gave his life a ranfom for many, was the great Author of univerfal Being, by whom all things were made, and in whom they confift, it was neceffary, for the defence and confirmation of the gofpel, that fufficient and credible witneffes fhould behold an emanation of that divine majefty, wherewith he had been from all eternity invefted, and which he only laid afide for the falvation of mankind. It was neceffary, that among thofe, who were to preach him to the world, fome fhould be found, who had actually feen, as far as might be permitted to mortals, the magnificence of his glorious Godhead.

More particularly was this neceffary, becaufe a fpectacle of a very different kind was fhortly to be prefented to their view. Their Mafter, their Benefactor, their Friend, was foon to be taken from them

them by sacrilegious violence. The day of our Saviour's life was far spent—the evening was at hand—he was about to close his work of mercy, and to offer up his spotless soul a ransom for sin. The hour was near in its approach, when human malice, combining with the powers of darkness, should prevail against the Redeemer of mankind.

For this severe trial it was the office of our blessed Lord to prepare his followers—some, by prophetic declaration of the event, and of his glorious resurrection which was to ensue—others, by pointing out to them that his kingdom was not of this world, and by exalting their hope to the regions of eternal joy—while to some he vouchsafed more immediate visions and revelations of God; when he took them into an high mountain apart, and was transfigured before them ; when his face did shine as the sun, and his raiment was bright as the light: when He,

He, who came not to deftroy, but to fulfil the law and the prophets, was attended by the immortal fpirits of the greateft of law-givers and firft of prophets—when they appeared in glory, and filled the beholders with extafy and with amazement.

In dwelling on this awful and myfterious fcene, it is impoffible not to recollect, that the departure of both Mofes and Elias from the world which they now vifited as celeftial beings, was not like that of common men. Elijah, (or Elias) in a whirlwind of fire, was tranflated to the regions of glory. Mofes, after he had fulfilled his miniftry, refigned his foul to his Creator; but apart from all witneffes. How he expired—where his remains were depofited—and what was the conteft between the enemy of mankind and the bleffed Archangel concerning him, all this is buried in impenetrable darknefs. However, a greater than

than Moses, a greater than Elias was here—and the law and the prophets did on this occasion avouch the preeminence of the Gospel, while Moses and Elias, their illustrious representatives, paid homage, and made obeisance to the Messiah.

In the midst of this assemblage of glory, what was the subject, on which the patriarch and prophet discoursed with the Son of God? They spake not of his eternal kingdom, his majesty, his sovereignty over all that is named in heaven and earth—they spake not of the adoration of angels, nor of the myriads of voices which cry, " Holy, Holy, " Holy, Lord God of Hosts:" *they spake of his decease.* Either to support and encourage the human nature of Christ, or to praise and magnify the unbounded mercy of his divine essence, they spake of his decease which he should accomplish at Jerusalem. They congratulated the

the conqueror of Sin and Death—and perhaps they animated him to perfift in his career of victory. And he, who on other occafions was ftrengthened by the miniftry of Angels, was now applauded by the Spirits of juft Men made perfect.

The effect of this aftonifhing vifion on the minds of the mortals who were permitted to behold it, muft tranfcend the utmoft limits of our comprehenfion. Their joy on this difplay of their Lord's glory, feems almoft too mighty for their natures to fuftain. While they lift up their eyes to this manifeftation of the divine Majefty, we hear them explain, in broken accents of rapture, " Mafter, " Mafter, it is good for us to be here"— nay they wifh, but in vain, to prolong the ftay of their immortal guefts. " *Let us make three tabernacles—one for thee, and one for Mofes, and one for Elias.*" Here let us dwell; here let us abide. One day, one moment in this bleffed fociety society is better than a thousand years spent in the enjoyment of all that mortals hold dear or desirable."

" While they yet spake, behold, a
" bright cloud over-shadowed them—
" and behold, a voice out of the cloud,
" which said, " This is my beloved Son,
" in whom I am well pleased—hear ye
" him !" The voice of God himself from Heaven bears witness to the Saviour of mankind; and the Apostles are confirmed in their faith by the Lord Omnipotent, thus proclaiming the divinity of Jesus Christ. St. Peter, at a remote period of time, speaks of the effect which this glorious attestation produced on those who heard it: and offers it to his converts as a most forcible argument, (What could indeed be more forcible ?) to establish and strengthen their faith. " For we have not followed cunningly-devised fables, when we made known unto you the power and coming of our Lord

The Transfiguration.

Lord Jesus Christ, but were eye-witnesses of his Majesty. For he received from God the Father honour and glory, when there came such a voice to him from the excellent glory, " This is my " beloved Son, in whom I am well pleas- " ed:" and this voice, that came from heaven, *we heard*, when we were with him in the holy mount."

And now the bright cloud disappears; the voice is past; the lawgiver and prophet return to the mansions of the blessed; and our Saviour gradually resumes that form, which veiled his divinity, while he appeared on earth, and conversed with men. Yet is it probable, that some remains of celestial glory irradiated his features; and that, as it happened unto Moses, after the revelations on Sinai, so, when our Lord came down from the mount, his countenance shone with more than mortal splendor: for the people, who had long been waiting for him, when they beheld him " *were greatly amazed,*

amazed, and running to him, faluted him." What might be the fource of their amazement we are left to conjecture : and furely the conjecture is by no means improbable, that his face, which fo lately did fhine as the fun, was not altogether and in a moment divefted of its luftre.

He returns to the multitude : he works a great and aftonifhing miracle, in a cafe which called for the exertion of his own power, having baffled that of his difciples: and then he imparts to thofe around him the leffon, which it is at this time my object to imprint on the hearts of my chriftian brethren———

" Let thefe fayings fink down into your ears : for the Son of Man fhall be betrayed into the hands of men." As if he had faid,

" Prepare yourfelves for the fcandal of the Crofs. Be not difmayed, or fhaken

in

in your faith, when you fee your mafter betrayed, tormented, bafely and malicioufly murdered. The foundations of that hope, which I came to infpire, are laid, not in time, but in eternity—not in earth, but in the Heaven of heavens. It is impoffible that one, who doeth the miracles ye fee me do, can be otherwife than divine. Let not your hearts be troubled: ye believe in God—believe alfo in me. And ye, my chofen difciples, to whom I have now vouchfafed a glimpfe of my *glory*, let it prepare you for the *agony* which ye fhall be called on to witnefs—and, in that awful and tremendous moment, remember the bright vifion on Mount Tabor*."

Let thefe fublime meditations increafe our Chriftian faith, and animate our hope—our faith in Him, who, though he came to vifit us in great humility,

---

* St. Jerome fays, that it was the general tradition of his day, that our Saviour was transfigured on *Mount Tabor*.

could thus, at his pleasure, array himself in majesty and glory; and our hope, that through his merits, when this mortal life shall be at an end, we shall be received into the presence of that Almighty Being, with whom do live the spirits of them that depart hence in the Lord, after they are delivered from their earthly prisons.

In Christ Jesus we behold the fulness of the law and of the prophets. We see Moses and Elias, coming from their state of blessedness to worship Him, through whom alone the heirs of immortality are made partakers of the divine nature, and of everlasting glory. And we feel the wisdom and the justice of those divine commands: "Let all the angels of God worship him : let every knee bow at the name of JESUS: let every tongue confess that he is Lord, to the glory of God the Father.

While

While we are thus admitted, as it were, within the veil, and behold a portion of the Holy of Holies—while that manifeſtation of the Divine Majeſty, which even its choſen witneſſes were for a time enjoined to conceal, is now clearly revealed unto us—how do our hearts diſclaim, how do they riſe ſuperior to all the low and baſe objects of mortal ambition or deſire! And when we conſider the infinite diſproportion between that ſcene, grand and magnificent as it was, and the full glories of that heavenly kingdom which it repreſented, how can we but ſay, in the rapture of our hearts, " LORD, *it is good for us to be* THERE !" Thither let our ſouls aſcend, and to their habitation let them come! We will ariſe and go to our Father—for in his preſence is the fulneſs of joy, and at his right hand there is pleaſure for evermore.

SERM.
IV.
And thou, O gracious Lord, whose most dearly beloved Son was manifested that he might make us the children of God, and heirs of immortal life; grant to us thy humble servants, that, having this hope, we may purify ourselves, even as he is pure—that when he shall appear again with power and great glory, we may be made like unto him in his eternal and glorious kingdom, where with thee, O Father, and thee O Holy Ghost, he liveth and reigneth, one GOD blessed for ever-more: to whom be ascribed, as is most due, all honour, power, might, majesty, and dominion, world without end. Amen.

SERMON

SERMON V.

THE ATONEMENT.

PREACHED ON GOOD-FRIDAY.

SERMON V.

THE ATONEMENT.

PSALM xxii.—1.

"*My God! My God! Why haſt thou forſaken me?*"

To recite theſe words is to apply them. Your hearts are gone already to Mount Calvary; and you behold with the eye of faith your crucified Redeemer. Lo, the rocks are rent—the mid-day ſun is plunged into obſcurity—the graves are opened—the ſaints who ſlept in death ariſe and appear—the frame of nature feels

feels as it were the pangs of diſſolution, while its Creator ſuffers.

When, on the return of this ſacred day, or at any other ſeaſon of devotion, we meditate on the paſſion of our Lord—when we accompany the innocent Jeſus through the horrors of his arraignment—through his unjuſt and mercileſs trial—when we witneſs the mockery and deſpitefulneſs of his triumphant enemies, the treachery, the defection, and the apoſtaſy of his diſciples——when we ſurvey the inſtruments of torture—the wreath of thorns, the bloody ſcourge—the ponderous croſs, under which his weakened, exhauſted nature fainted and almoſt ſank away—when we view him faſtened to the engine of death—his hands and his feet transfixed with the nails—the iron entering into his ſoul—his bleſſed ſide pierced by wanton, officious cruelty—when we behold all this, how little do we comprehend the extent of our Saviour's anguiſh, how

how imperfectly do we conceive the bitterness of his cup, if we do not keep always in our view the leading feature in his paffion, the woe of all woes, the terrors of God fet in array againft him, the wrath of his Father heavy upon him, the confummate guilt of a world, heaped upon his guiltlefs head!

This, my brethren, was the torment worfe than death—this it was, which made our bleffed Saviour fo pre-eminently "acquainted with grief." Acute, painful, exquifite, as were the fufferings of his body, they were fufferings fuch as (in a variety of inftances) mere mortals, through affifting grace, had before, and have fince, endured with conftancy— nay many who were not in poffeffion of refources like thofe of the martyr in the hour of trial, have, by ftrength of body or mind, in ancient and in modern times, furmounted them. Surely then, if death, in ever fo horrid a form, was

all

SERM. V.

all which our Lord, (a divine, a voluntary victim), had to sustain, we should not have heard him utter this doleful and passionate exclamation, " *My* God! " *My* God! *why hast thou forsaken me?*" But view the case in its true light—behold the Mediator between God and man, for the sins of man, suffering in his human nature a temporary exclusion from the face of God—view him wounded for our offences, and bruised for our iniquities—see him stricken, smitten of God, and afflicted—think on the intolerable burden thus laid upon him, and you will no longer wonder at the intenseness of his anguish. " Is it nothing " to you, all ye that pass by? Behold " and see, if there be any sorrow like " unto my sorrow, which HE hath done " unto me, wherewith THE LORD hath " afflicted me, in the day of his fierce " anger." While our Redeemer could hold communication with heaven, neither the cruel ingratitude of mankind, nor the

the miseries of every description which he sustained during his life, nor the blasphemy of the multitude in the hour of his death, nor the scourge, nor the thorns, nor the cross itself, could shake his constancy. But when a dark cloud was interposed between our Lord, and the Almighty Father of Light—when he, who had long since been forsaken by man, appeared for a while to be forsaken by God, then, then was the measure of his sufferings complete: then he spake in the bitterness of his soul; he complained, for his spirit was overwhelmed.

With the foretaste of this unutterable woe was the heart of our Saviour filled, when he sought for some alleviation, by communicating his sufferings to his helpless, feeble, astonished disciples. "My " soul is exceeding sorrowful unto " death!"—It was with a reference to this

this extremity of grief, that in the days of his flesh with strong crying and tears he prayed, that, if it were possible, the hour might pass from him—" Abba, " Father, all things are possible to thee; " take away *this* cup from me: nevertheless not my will, but thine be done!" The will of God *was* done: the cup, with all its bitterness, was drunk to the very dregs, that so the sacrifice might be made efficient for the sins of the whole world: but during this grievous conflict an angel appeared from Heaven, strengthening him. He rose, invigorated by these communications from above; he delivered himself, with unresisting meekness, into the hands of his enemies. He was arraigned—he was crucified—he made atonement for our sins— he underwent the wrath of God—he then cried, " It is finished. Father, into " thy hands I commend my spirit;" and, having said thus, he yielded up the ghost.

That

That face, which had been hidden from him for a feafon, beamed again with its divine effulgence on the Redeemer of mankind, when, every prophecy being fulfilled, every type accomplifhed, every fatisfaction for the mighty debt fully difcharged, he refigned his departing fpirit into the arms of a reconciled Father—reconciled to a world of finners, who had fome time been alienated, and enemies in their mind by wicked works, yet who now were enabled to prefent themfelves in the garments of a Saviour's righteoufnefs, holy, and unblameable, and unreproveable in the fight of God.

Having contemplated the fufferings of our bleffed Redeemer in this their confummation, let us review fome of the *preparatory* circumftances which led to thofe fufferings. They will ftill more clearly explain to us the meaning of that exclamation of grief, which burft from the

the heart of the divine Sufferer, " My ".God! my God! why haft *thou* for-" faken me!"

Nothing is more certain, than that our Saviour had a perfect foreknowledge of every event which was to befal him. For this was he born, and for this caufe came he into the world, that he might give his life a ranfom for many. We hear thefe ftriking declarations from his own facred lips: " Therefore doth the Father love me, becaufe I lay down my life— no man taketh it from me; but I lay it down of myfelf. Behold, we go up to Jerufalem; and the Son of Man fhall be betrayed unto the chief priefts, and unto the fcribes, and they fhall condemn him to death, and fhall deliver him to the Gentiles to mock, and to fcourge, and to crucify him." Though every forrow which he had to fuftain was thus prefent to his view, his love for mankind, stronger than death, led him to expect all
without

without regret or repining, save the horror of that moment, when the Lord laid on him the iniquities of us all. If we consider his actions with a reference to every other torment which he endured, we find him stedfast and immoveable, unappalled by suffering, and superior to pain: we behold him administering comfort, and healing the broken-hearted, even to the very moment of his agony. " Ye now therefore have sorrow," saith he to his afflicted disciples; " but I will see you again, and your heart shall rejoice, and your joy no man taketh from you." While he stood before the tribunal of an unjust judge, who thirsted for his blood, and was determined on the perpetration of murder, he could bestow a look of pity, of affection, of kind remembrance, of parental remonstrance, on that wretched apostle, who, aghast and panic-struck, was heaping crime upon crime, and, to escape a momentary danger, was preparing for himself long and bitter remorse. While on the way to his crucifixion, he mourned, not for himself, but for the dangers impending over a guilty and miserable people: " Weep not for me, but weep for your- " selves, and for your children, ye daugh- " ters of Jerusalem." When his eyes were well-nigh closed in death, his inextinguishable filial love directed itself to assuage the sorrows of his agonizing mother, into whose soul the prophesied sword was then infixed; at that moment, in accents of pious tenderness, he consigned her to the care of his beloved disciple. One act of mercy remained to be performed, and mark how the Saviour of mankind accomplished it! Mark how the promise of peace, and life, and pardon, was uttered by his gracious lips, and revived the soul of a contrite offender: Verily I say to thee, " This day shalt " thou be with me in Paradise."

We

We have seen then that our blessed Lord became a voluntary sacrifice for us men and for our salvation, that by his death he might destroy the power of death: but to be deprived of his Father's presence—to exchange that unutterable glory with which he had been invested before the foundation of the world, not only for the scorn of men, but for the wrath of God—this was an extremity of anguish, that not even the power of Christ himself in his human nature could sustain without a struggle, the severity of which no language can adequately express, no thought can adequately conceive.

To excite your gratitude to your beneficent Redeemer for blessings so inestimable—to fill your hearts with a sense of the divine benignity of Christ who died for you—to inspire you with a just abhorrence of sin, which called for such an expiation—to impress on your minds

SERM.
V.

a fenfe of the value of thofe immortal fouls, the ranfom of which could not be effected but by an oblation fo precious—to warn you of the danger of difobedience, and the fenfelefs infatuation of cafting away the high privilege of your redemption—to remind you that it is vain for you to profefs that you love God, if you keep not his commandments—and to exhort you, as you regard your own falvation, to improve the time of probation allotted you, and to feek after God while he may be found—all thefe obvious inferences from the holy folemnity of this day, it is the conftant office of the minifter of Chrift to inculcate on its annual return. But the fubject is inexhauftible : it is infinite as the divine bounty in which it originates.

And now, if there be any here, whom it has pleafed God, for wife and good reafons, to try in the furnace of affliction—if there be any from whom he
has

has seemed to hide his blessed face, and to turn away his ear, as though he regarded not their piercing cries; let them remember, that thus, even thus, the pure and innocent Jesus was contented to suffer, when he visited us in great humility. Let their wounded spirit be cheered by the reflection, that the God whom they serve will not contend for ever, will not be always wroth: he will turn again, he will have compassion on his servants, he will forgive all their iniquities, and cast their sins into the depths of the sea; again will he cause his face to shine upon them, and they shall be saved. " Heaviness may endure for a night"—it may even accompany them till they descend into the dark and silent tomb—" but joy cometh in the morning." The day will dawn—the shadows will fly away—the glorious light of righteousness will arise upon them; and their temporary afflictions shall be rewarded

warded by an exceeding and eternal weight of glory.

Encouraged by this bleſſed hope, the Chriſtian prepares himſelf for the evils which may await him, and abides in humble reſignation till the calamity be overpaſt. He takes up his croſs, and follows the example of his Saviour—he remembers his Redeemer's ſorrows, and he is triumphant over his own. "O glorious
" Captain of our ſalvation, who didſt
" firſt ſuffer many things, and then en-
" teredſt into thy glory; ſanctify to us
" all the pains of body, and all the ter-
" rors of mind which thou ſhalt at any
" time permit to fall upon us: and make
" us ſo patiently to ſuffer with thee here,
" that we may alſo be glorified eternally
" with thee hereafter * !"

One more obſervation of the moſt intereſting nature, preſſes itſelf irreſiſtibly

* See Hele's Devotions, p. 304.

on

on the mind. I shall mention it, and dismiss you.

When our Saviour, in his bitter anguish, called on the Almighty with earnest expostulation, he adopted the pathetic language of his royal ancestor, saying, "My God! my God! why hast "thou forsaken me*?" Again, when (having expiated our sins) he was about to enter into his rest, he remembered the words of the holy Psalmist: and, as I have already pointed out to you, concluded his glorious course by thus addressing his Almighty Father; "into thy hands I commend my spirit †." O let not the force of our Lord's example be lost upon us! Let the word of God be ever in our hearts—let us meditate therein day and night—let us constantly search the scripture for language in which we may give utterance to our prayers, and

* Psalm xxii. 1.   † Psalm xxxi. 6.

to our praifes. It is very meet, right, and our bounden duty, that we fhould at all times, and in all places, in all fituations, and on all occafions, in health and in ficknefs, in joy and in forrow, in profperity and in adverfity, in youth and in age—that to the very lateft moment of our exiftence, as long as we retain the power of fpeech, as long as one tongue can perform its office, we fhould have recourfe to the fongs of Sion. They will footh the departing fpirit. They will teach it to wing its flight towards heaven. They will put it in preparation for the melody of Angels, when, in the glorious morning of the Refurrection, our triumphant Saviour will put a new fong into our mouths, a new thankfgiving unto our God.

SERMON

SERMON VI.

THE STATE OF THE DEPARTED.

SERMON VI.

THE STATE OF THE DEPARTED.

ZECHARIAH i.—5.

Your fathers, where are they?

THE answer to this demand of the prophet is a very solemn one. "They "have left the world, and are now in "their respective graves, where they "shall rest, till the trump of God shall "summon them to everlasting judgement. "Then, standing before his dreadful "tribunal,

SERM.
VI.

"tribunal, they shall each receive the righteous sentence, according to that they have done, whether it be good or bad. In the mean time, they are in that invisible world, whither we and our children shall follow them; nor is it more certain that they once lived, than that we shall likewise die."

What a variety of reflections are presented to the soul, when we contemplate the ages that are past! What useful and instructive lessons are thus to be learned, if we will but dispose our hearts to receive conviction! The subject animates, though it affects us—if for a moment it should cast a gloom over our minds, the hope which is set before us affords us ample amends—if it places the image of death before our eyes, it directs our faith to him, who himself entered the dreadful lists with the enemy of mankind, and delivered them, who through fear of death would otherwise have

have been all their life-time subject unto bondage.

From the question in my text, and the reply which faith enables us to make, I shall direct your attention to the following particulars:

I. The insufficiency of human projects and designs.

II. The certainty of a future resurrection to judgement.

III. The necessity of "leading a godly and christian life," if we would die the death of the righteous.

First, Our thoughts on the approach we all are making towards the grave, set before us in the strongest light the insufficiency of those projects which are formed by short-lived, fallible mortals.

"*Go*

"*Go to now*," faith the apoftle, "*ye that fay, to-day or to-morrow we will go into fuch a city, and continue there a year, and buy, and fell, and get gain. Whereas ye know not what fhall be on the morrow. For what is your life? It is even a vapour, that appeareth for a little time, and then vanifheth away.*" The confideration of the fhortnefs of life forbids our laying too great a ftrefs on vifionary plans of worldly advantage, left, in the midft of our defigns, we fhall be called upon to join the multitude of departed fouls, while unprepared in the greateft and moft folemn of all concerns.

I am aware, that a fpirit of enterprize may have its ufe—and that, as well as a criminal, there is a laudable ambition in the human mind, which ought not to be fuppreffed. Let not therefore the energies of the foul be weakened; let not the arm of honeft induftry be checked in its

its exertions: but in all our actions, in all our endeavours, let us, with a due sense of our own infirmity (creatures as we are of an hour) submit ourselves and our hopes to the Author and Giver of our being: *If the Lord will, we shall live and do this or that.* We are not commanded to be idle; but, whatsoever we do, to do it in the name of our Lord Jesus Christ. Our best interests thus secured, should death interrupt us in the prosecution of our designs, still are we the Lord's. Those who are departed hence in his faith and fear can never at any period be said to have left the world before their time. Some of these faithful servants of their Lord had perhaps, in the course of nature, many years of health and vigour in prospect—but God, who had proved them and found them worthy of himself, in the midst of their pilgrimage deemed them ripe for glory, and consigned them to the mansions of rest, and peace, and everlasting joy. Do you imagine, my brethren,

SERM. VI.

brethren, thefe glorified fpirits lament, that they have left fome project unaccomplifhed, fome defign imperfectly executed on earth, when they fee the eternal gates of Heaven opening to receive them, and hear their Redeemer's voice, calling them to the participation of thofe bright rewards, which his own precious bood-fhedding procured for them?

Our ignorance of what is to happen to us in future affords another argument, in addition to that deduced from the fhortnefs of human life, to check our too eager purfuits of fublunary enjoyments. How can we, under fuch circumftances, prefume to devote our time, our thoughts, our faculties, to projects flow in their operation, uncertain in their fuccefs, and diftant in their accomplifhment? Who knoweth what is good for man in this life, all the days of his vain life which he fpendeth as a fhadow? Of what is to come we all know nothing—a dark a dark, an impenetrable veil hangs over the remainder of our days.

Far be it from my thoughts to call in queſtion the procedure of divine providence. Here, as in all his other dealings with mankind, our heavenly Father ordereth the concerns of his children with parental mercy. Could we know beforehand of the misfortunes that may befal us, exiſtence would, in ſome inſtances, be an inſupportable burthen: whereas hope now caſts a gleam of ſunſhine athwart theſe hours, which would otherwiſe have been paſt in gloomy preſages of ſorrow; many a gracious interval of ſerenity enables us to recover our ſtrength before the tempeſt is again ſtirred up round about us; and though the winds rage, the rains deſcend, and the floods ſwell, we truſt in the mercy of our God, and abide the horror of the dark and cloudy day.

Again,

Again. The experience of what has paffed, fhould warn and admonifh us in future. Our fathers had their plans and defigns; they bought, they fold, they planted, they builded; and, fo far as in thefe occupations they ferved their generation, they fulfilled the will of God: but in thefe purfuits fome of them ferved the creature more than the Creator; they forgat God their Saviour; they purfued unreal phantoms of vifionary greatnefs, and in the pride of their hearts exclaimed, " To-morrow fhall be as this day, " and much more abundant." Yet now, where are they? How are they loft in oblivion! In the grave the ambitious and the humble, the turbulent and peaceable, lie down together, and for the moft part are heard of no more—unlefs their actions have obtained them a place in the recording page of hiftory, which is more frequently a regifter of human vice, and of human barbarity, than a pleafing memorial of what-
foever

soever things are true—whatsoever things are honest—whatsoever things are pure, lovely, and of good report.

Let us for a moment suppose, that those persons, after whom the prophet enquires, could stand before us: that the multitude of departed spirits—the characters of antiquity—our own ancestors among the number—could rise from their several tombs, and address us: Gracious heaven, what a sermon would they preach!

II. And rise they most certainly shall. The awful scene is not imaginary. A day will come—we appeal to the word of God for the truth of what we say—when " all that are in the grave shall " hear His voice," shall stand forth, and shall appear before him. Wherever our fathers are now, we know that they shall then assemble at the judgement-seat of Christ—whether their remains now lie in the remoteſt parts of the habitable world, or whether they were committed to the boſom of the deep, it matters not. *Space*, as well as *time*, ſhall be no more. When the Son of God ſhall come with power and great glory, " before him " ſhall be gathered all nations." Then, amidſt that countleſs multitude, ſhall we, and our children, and our fathers, await the righteous ſentence which ſhall proceed out of his mouth. In that ſolemn hour, thoſe decrees of Providence, which now ſeem myſterious, and which are beyond the reach of human comprehenſion, will appear to have been ordered by unerring Wiſdom and infinite Juſtice; and all mankind ſhall bow down with humble ſubmiſſion before God, crying out, in accents of adoration, " Thou art righteous, O Lord, in all " thy ways, and holy in all thy works!" Then ſhall oppreſſed innocence lift up its head with joy, no longer expoſed to the fury of the oppreſſor. Thoſe tears,

which

which have flowed down the cheek of the poor and deftitute, fhall be wiped away for ever from their eyes—the proud enemies of God, who had their vain triumph on earth for a time, fhall know againft whom they dared to exalt themfelves—all that feemed to the mortal fenfe as difcord, fhall appear to have been conducive and preparatory to everlafting harmony.

With the circumftances which fhall attend on that awful day, it has pleafed God, in his wifdom, to acquaint us, and by his divine revelation to imprefs our minds with a due fenfe of its certainty, and of its folemnity. It may, however, be remarked, that though the terrors of the Lord are occafionally fet before our view, the voice of infpiration, even on this momentous fubject, rather animates our hopes, than awakens our fears. Let us in this light confider each of the particular defcriptions of Chrift's fecond coming, which are handed down to us in the oracles of truth.

In the firſt of theſe * our Lord himſelf reveals to his diſciples the manner of his future coming—the ſeparation of the wicked from the juſt—the trial both of the one and the other; and their adjudication to everlaſting puniſhment, or to life eternal. Nothing can be imagined more truly awful; nor can all the powers of eloquence come in competition with its majeſtic ſublimity. We ſee the whole world ſtanding before the tribunal—Chriſt himſelf the Judge, arrayed in all the glory of the omnipotent God—heaven his throne—earth his footſtool—innumerable multitudes of angels, the miniſters of his judgement, and of his mercy.

The ſecond paſſage of ſcripture alluded to, is the memorable account of

* Matt. xxv. 31, &c.

the Refurrection, as delivered by St. Paul to his Corinthian converts *. It is the voice of comfort, of hope, of joy in the midſt of ſorrow. It is the triumph of Faith over death and the grave. Chriſt's refurrection, as leading to ours—the myſterious exchange from mortality to glory, when the laſt trumpet ſhall ſound—the future incorruptible ſtate of thoſe, who are now ſleeping in Chriſt—the ſting of death plucked out—the power of the grave overthrown—all is ſet before our eyes in ſuch ſtrong and lively colours, that our hearts echo the ſong of exultation, and we are led to exclaim, with the inſpired apoſtle, " Thanks be " to God, who giveth us the victory, " through our Lord Jeſus Chriſt."

The laſt paſſage alluded to I ſhall recite at length, requeſting you, at the

---

* 1 Cor. xv.

same time, to keep in your minds what has been said, that the voice of Religion is the voice of Joy. *"I would not have you to be ignorant, brethren, concerning them which are asleep, that ye sorrow not, even as others, which have no hope. For if we believe that Jesus died and rose again, even so them also which sleep in Jesus will God bring with him. For this we say unto you by the word of the Lord, that we which are alive and remain unto the coming of the Lord shall not prevent them which are asleep. For the Lord himself shall descend from heaven with a shout, with the voice of the Archangel, and with the trump of God; and the dead in Christ shall rise first. Then we which are alive and remain, shall be caught up together with them in the clouds to meet the Lord in the air; and so shall we ever be with the Lord*—WHEREFORE COMFORT ONE ANOTHER WITH THESE WORDS*."

* 1 Thess. iv. 14, &c.

3. The

3. The question then, as far as it respected our fathers, is fully answered. They sleep in death; they shall awake to judgment. But this is not a subject of barren and useless speculation; it has its fruit unto holiness, if we apply to *ourselves* every particular of what has been said.

Our fathers are departed from the world. They had their season of probation — we are at this time passing through ours. The event which has taken place with respect to them awaits all of us in our turn. "It is appointed unto all men once to die." The most consummate wisdom cannot devise any expedient to avert the sentence—honours, riches, power, cannot avail to defer its accomplishment. Let us remember then (and be this the inference from all that has been said), that here we have no continuing city—that we are subject to the same immutable laws as

SERM. VI.

were our fathers—that we hold our lives on the fame tenure by which they held theirs—that we fhall be called upon to leave this world, whether it is to us a world of joys or of forrows—that we fhall join the company of departed fpirits; and that our children, rifing up in our ftead, fhall, in due time, fubmit to the inevitable decree themfelves. They will probably enquire, with fome curiofity, after us, their anceftors. If our vices or follies come to their ears, our names will not efcape the feverity of reproach. If our virtues have entitled us to their remembrance, a tear of pious gratitude fhall embalm our lifelefs remains.

But motives of a fuperior nature call upon us to live foberly, righteoufly, and godly, in this prefent world. As we employ the fpace of time allotted us here, fo fhall we be happy or miferable hereafter. The duties are plain. The rewards

rewards propofed are glorious. The dangers we have to expect are pointed out to us by the finger of God: and we are promifed his fupport, that we may be enabled to overcome them. While we have light, therefore, let us walk in the light, that we may be the children of the light. Let the confideration of the fhortnefs and the viciffitude of human life teach us to place our fure truft in the Author of our falvation, the Lord Jefus Chrift—who, having vifited the earth in great humility, and having himfelf tafted of death, is now exalted at the right hand of the throne of God. And let me befeech you, in his name, and for his fake, to walk worthy of the vocation wherewith ye are called. He is the Refurrection and the Life. If ye believe in him, though ye be dead, yet fhall ye live: for whofoever liveth and believeth in him fhall never die. Though you fall, you fhall not be caft down, for the Lord will uphold you

with

SERM. VI.

with his hand. Your hope shall be full of immortality. God will make you partakers of the inheritance of the saints in light: He, whom ye have loved, and under whose banners ye have fought, shall welcome you to the participation of everlasting glory.

In the mean time, your memorial shall be sacred even on earth—your children, and your children's children, shall arise and call you blessed. Your virtues shall take root in an honourable soil—they shall spring up from the ground, and blossom from the dust. And when the question in my text is put to your posterity, " *Your fathers, where are* " *they?*" They will reply, with generous elation of soul, " THEIR BODIES ARE " BURIED IN PEACE: BUT THEIR NAME " LIVETH FOR EVER AND EVER."

SERMON

SERMON VII.

THE NAME OF GOD GLORIFIED.

SERMON VII.

THE NAME OF GOD GLORIFIED.

JOHN xii.—28.

"Father, glorify thy name!" Then came there a voice from heaven, saying, "I have both glorified it, and will glorify it again."

IN the words before us, Chrift, the Son of God, calls to his eternal Father; and the Father anfwers from his celeftial throne. There is fomething uncommonly fublime and interefting in this open

open manifest converse between the human nature incarnate, and the divine essence from which that human nature flowed, seated in everlasting Majesty. "Father, glorify thy name." "I have both glorified it, and will glorify it again."

To enter into the full spirit and meaning of these memorable words, we must have recourse to the preceding verses, uttered by the Saviour of mankind soon after his most signal display of power, in the restoration of Lazarus from the tomb, to which he had for three days been consigned—an act, not only marvellous in itself, but prefiguring evidently the accomplishment of his often-repeated prophecy concerning his own resurrection. His implacable enemies, exasperated rather than convinced, by such a manifest demonstration that he was sent from God, were now more resolutely bent on his destruction; and to remove from

from the eyes of the people the living witnefs of Chrift's omnipotence, they "confulted to put Lazarus alfo to death—" to fend him back by martyrdom to that grave, whence he had been recalled by miracle.

The paffover was at hand; and the chief priefts determined, if Jefus affifted at its folemnities, to take fome occafion againft him which might affect his life, and to find fome plaufible pretence for fhedding the precious blood of the Lamb of God. How were their impious hopes for a time difappointed by the loud hofannahs of the multitude, welcoming the Lord of Life to his own holy temple, when he came to make the glory of the latter houfe greater than that of the former! "Perceive ye," faid the Pharifees, "how ye prevail nothing? behold, the "world is gone after him."

Alas,

SERM. VII.

Alas, who can rely, for one short moment, on the stability of popular applause? What meant these loud hosannahs, this joyful homage to the Son of David, so soon to be succeeded by the savage and discordant cry of, "Crucify him, Crucify him!" Thus, even thus, was it in the case of his royal progenitor. We see that holy patriarch triumphantly introduced into Jerusalem with shouting, and with the sound of a trumpet: but soon, by a sad reverse, the hearts of the men of Israel were after Absalom, and "David went up by the ascent of mount Olivet, and wept as he went up, and had his head covered, and he went barefoot."

Our Saviour foresaw a similar destiny to himself. He knew that the hour was near in its approach, in which the iniquity of a world would be laid upon his guiltless head. He knew what sacrifice was necessary for man's salvation. He com-

comprehended the extent of his sufferings, and he refolved to endure them. With an intrepidity worthy of the caufe which infpired it, he refigned himfelf to the will of heaven. "Now is my foul "troubled—and what fhall I fay? Fa- "ther, fave me from this hour?—But "for this caufe came I unto this hour. "Father, glorify thy name!" As if he had faid, "Amidft the acclamations of the multitude, even now, while they are fhouting for joy, and hailing me as the Redeemer of Ifrael, I am prepared for all things that fhall come upon me. Human nature revolts with horror from the idea of fuch tortures; and *my foul is troubled* at the contemplation of them. *But what fhall I fay?* fhall I deprecate the fufferings, which I offered myfelf, a willing victim, to fuftain? Shall I, in the very moment when I am preparing for this mighty conteft, lofe fight of the high prize which is to be procured by it, the deliverance of a finful world? Shall I have

have recourse to the omnipotence of my Father? Shall I fly to his everlasting arms for my protection, and there, at a distance from all possible danger, behold the progress of the storm which would then overwhelm the world in inevitable ruin? Not so, O my God, be thy tender mercies frustrated—not so be the purpose of thy grace disappointed! *For this cause came I unto this hour.* I came to suffer and to die; I came, that the warfare of all men might be accomplished, that their iniquity might be pardoned. Were I now to decline the momentous conflict, how should the divine wrath be appeased? how should the power of sin be destroyed? how should the kingdom of heaven be opened to all believers? " *Father, glorify thy name!*" Fulfil thy gracious designs— cause the voice of salvation to be heard —accept the atonement of innocence as a ransom for guilt. Lo, I come to do thy will, O God. Behold the Lamb for a burnt-offering!" To

To this effect spake the Messiah, while his heart, full of unbounded love towards mankind, prepared itself for the bitterness of death. The Almighty heard, and replied. It was a reply, not made according to the accustomed procedure of those communications from above, with which the Father held converse with his Son—it was not the " still small voice," whereby the Saviour of men was from time to time animated and encouraged to proceed in the work of mercy he had undertaken; such as we may presume he often heard in those solemn retirements, when prayer and praise to God employed him in the night-season. It was a full, public, decisive testimony from the Lord God omnipotent to the Son of man. The prayer of faith reacheth the clouds—it is heard even in " the secret place of thunder." While the people stood in reverential silence, listening to the words of their mighty prophet, as he called on Jehovah to glorify

SERM. VII.

his holy name, Lo, a voice from heaven, saying, "I have both glorified it, and will glorify it again." The God of Israel is either, as the Scripture expresses it, "a God that hideth himself," or he is a God that manifests himself openly, as his wisdom thinks best for the purposes of his divine Providence. And he, who had before glorified, and would hereafter glorify his name, did now, at the moment in which he spake, fully and completely glorify it—while in no mortal accents, but in words, such as they who indistinctly heard the sound, imagined to be the voice of an angel, or the majestic voice of thunder, he answered the prayer of his beloved Son.

To attempt at a recapitulation of those acts, whereby the Almighty, from the commencement of time to the hour in which this voice was heard, had glorified his holy name, is a task, the accomplishment of which exceeds the tongue of of men and of angels. Known unto God, and unto God only, are all his works from the beginning of the world. Can man, by searching, find them out? Can he discern them to perfection? They are higher than heaven—they are deeper than the foundations of the world—the measure of them is broader than the earth, and wider than the sea. Yet, as far as it was permitted to any mortals to comprehend his power, the highly-favoured people of Judah, beyond all others, knew the knowledge of the Most High. He dealt not with any nation as he had dealt with them—none, like them, were able to speak of his greatness. They had heard with their ears, and their fathers had told them, what works the Almighty had done in their days of old. In addition to the general manifestations of divine power, which had been shewn to all the world, they had peculiarly to record " his marvellous and strange wonders" displayed

SERM. VII. in their behalf. The call of their forefather Abraham—the bleſſing promiſed to his poſterity—the ſtupendous miracles wrought for the children of Iſrael by the arm of omnipotence during their abode in Egypt—the ſame Almighty arm extended in their defence, as he led them through the deep, and through the wilderneſs—his mercy exhibited in the full performance of his promiſe, when he brought his people with joy into the fertile Canaan—their inheritance in the land that flowed with milk and honey—their expulſion and exile from their country by reaſon of ſin ; and their reſtoration to the hill of Sion upon their true repentance—all, all went forcibly to their hearts—all bade them, with one accord, aſcribe glory to the Almighty. The voice ſpake unto them, as it were from heaven, " O magnify the Lord your God, and worſhip at his holy hill—for the Lord your God is holy."

While

While the declaration of the Almighty, "that he had glorified his name," had a reference to the mighty works we have been reciting, the promise "that he would glorify it yet again," had in view that great event, now about to be brought to its completion, the propitiatory sufferings of Jesus Christ. The glory which would be ascribed to Jehovah by the salvation of his people, was in the divine foreknowledge—the atonement for sin—the triumphs of the Gospel—the establishment of the kingdom of God—the Christian Church, small and inconsiderable in its beginning, but in its progress great, and reaching up to heaven; by means of which, the truth, in all its purity, would be revealed to the world, and faith, and knowlege, and repentance, and hope, would point out the way to a glorious immortality. Thus did God bear witness to his own dispensation; and thus the blessed Jesus (who was made a little lower than the angels,

for

for the suffering of death) was crowned with glory and honour, that he, by the grace of God, should taste death for every man. For it became him, for whom are all things, and by whom are all things, in bringing many sons unto glory, to make the Captain of their salvation perfect through sufferings—who himself, at the moment when the traitor Judas went to betray him, said, " Now is the son of man GLORIFIED, and God is glorified in him."

The Lamb of God, to whom his Father spake, well knew what was the import of the words. While the people, lost in amazement at the miraculous revelation from heaven, saw nothing but the exaltation of Christ, he foresaw his approaching passion. The cross was in his view, and the crown of thorns, which was to precede the crown of glory. He knew that he should triumph—but he knew that he must pass through the grave

grave and gate of death to his glorious refurrection. In this fenfe, enter into the full meaning of the words following my text. "Jefus anfwered and faid, *This voice came not, becaufe of me, but for your fakes. Now is the judgement of this world; now fhall the prince of this world be caft out; and I, if I be lifted up from the earth, will draw all men unto me.* This he faid, fignifying what death he fhould die."

But while he thus forefaw the conflict, he forefaw likewife the victory. For the joy that was fet before him, he endured the crofs, defpifing the fhame. With the painful and ignominious death he was to fuffer, he blended, in his prophetic mind, the power and majefty of his refurrection—his triumphs over the enemies of mankind—his afcent into heaven, and his return to the kingdom of his Father—the effufion of the Holy Ghoft upon

upon his chosen people—the radiant light of the everlasting Gospel.

He foresaw too, what in language becoming the subject he often foretold, the great, the future, the conclusive demonstration of his Almighty Power, which will hereafter most surely be displayed to all the world—when the Son of man shall come from heaven to earth, in like manner, as, in the presence of his admiring disciples, he ascended from earth to heaven: when the human nature of Christ, to whom all judgement is committed, shall pronounce sentence on the quick and dead; and, after that last act of the divine filiation, shall be for ever absorbed in the effulgence of the glorious Godhead.

The Almighty hath said, and shall he not do it? He hath spoken, and shall he not make it good? He hath glorified his name, and he will glorify it again.

For

For the Lord Jesus, who was taken up in a cloud to his glory, shall return in the clouds of heaven; and every eye shall see him. Then will God in all things be glorified through Jesus Christ. He will be glorified by the homage of universal nature, bowing before his majestic presence. He will be glorified in the dissolution of an expiring world. He will be glorified by all who shall be alive in the day of his coming, and who, having never slept in death, shall be changed in a moment, in the twinkling of an eye, at the last trump. He will be glorified by that display of sovereign power, which shall restore the souls of men to the bodies they once inhabited, calling on the dead to arise from their graves, and in their flesh to see God. He will be glorified in his righteous decrees, wherein all that hath been obscure shall be made plain, all that hath been mysterious shall be elucidated.

elucidated. He will be glorified by the rewards of once suffering virtue: by the joy wherewith they who have sorrowed for his sake shall be filled, and the comfort wherewith they shall be comforted. He will be glorified by the just, though tremendous, doom, which shall overwhelm the ungodly and impenitent: by the vindication of that power which they despised, of that omnipotence against which they madly boasted themselves. He will be glorified by the adoration of innumerable angels. He will be glorified by the hallelujahs of just men made perfect. He will be glorified in judgement—He will be glorified in mercy—He will be glorified by all that is in heaven, and all that is in earth, and all that is under the earth—and every tongue shall confess that Jesus Christ is Lord, to the glory of God the Father———

To whom, with the divine and co-eternal Spirit, three Persons and one God,

God, be afcribed, as is moft due, by the Church militant on earth, and the Church triumphant in heaven, all glory, honour, might, majefty, and dominion, from generation to generation. Amen.

SERMON

SERMON VIII.

THE VANITY OF HUMAN WISHES.

Nil ergo optabunt homines? Si confilium vis,
Permittes ipfis expendere Numinibus, quid
Conveniat nobis, rebufque fit utile noftris.
Nam, pro jucundis, aptiffima quæque dabunt Dii.
Carior eft illis homo, quam fibi.

         Juv. Sat. x. 346.

SERMON VIII.

THE VANITY OF HUMAN WISHES.

JOB vi.—8, 9.

Oh that I might have my request, and that God would grant me the thing that I long for,

Even that it would please God to destroy me!

THUS spake the man, who was distinguished, above all other human beings, for his sufferings, and for his patience. But he spake it in the bitterness of his soul—he spake it, without duly weighing its import, or the consequences of what

what he uttered. It was for this, and other expreſſions of the ſame tendency, which his unheard-of ſorrows forced from him, that he was reproved, not only by his ſevere and mercileſs friends, but by the juſt and impartial Elihu—by the awful voice of God. Senſible of his fault, he repents in duſt and aſhes. " Behold, I am vile—what ſhall I ſay unto thee ? I will lay my hand upon my mouth. Once have I ſpoken, but I will not anſwer—yea, twice—but I will proceed no further."

Let it not be argued, therefore, from the example of this eminent ſaint of God, that, even in caſes of extreme adverſity and affliction, it is lawful for us to murmur, or complain, or to diſpute with divine Providence; much leſs that it is permitted us to expreſs any undue anxiety to be relieved from our ſufferings by the ſtroke of death. We muſt wait for God's own time, and, until the arrival of of it, we muſt bear the burden of our misfortunes, whatever they be. He who begins to wiſh, and to pray for diſſolution, is in a ſtate of no inconſiderable danger: one ſtep more, and he will contend for the lawfulneſs and expediency of haſtening the time of his departure—another, and he will carry his pernicious principle into effect, and become himſelf the executioner of vengeance on his own wretched head.

But it is not my deſign to expatiate on a ſubject, on which there can be no diſſentient voice among thoſe who are in poſſeſſion of ſound reaſon, or of Chriſtian faith. My preſent purpoſe is rather to ſtate the vanity of human wiſhes—their probable tendency—our ignorance in aſking—God's all-perfect knowledge—and the duty incumbent on us to commit ourſelves entirely to the protection of his good Providence: while we humbly beſeech his mercy " to put away from us all

all hurtful things, and to give us those things which may be profitable for us, through Jesus Christ our Lord."

" O that I might have my request, " and that God would grant me the " thing that I long for!" It has been the voice of frail and short-sighted man, from the moment of his creation to the present hour. Too frequently do we presume to think ourselves wiser than our Maker, and better qualified to decide on what shall tend to our happiness. Besides all that God has given us, we are still presumptuously seeking for more. Some unpossessed object flits before our eyes, and allures us far away from the real good we might enjoy. Ingenious contrivers of our own uneasiness, we take care to fix on something out of our reach—perhaps, for our greater torment, almost, though not altogether, in our grasp—and then we forget all the blessings vouchsafed to us—we fret, and pine,

The Vanity of Human Wishes. SERM. VIII.

pine, and murmur, the froward, querulous victims of folly and impatience.

The fruit of the tree of knowledge was the object of our first parents' wishes. Not contented with that portion of wisdom which the Almighty knew to be most conducive to their happiness, they sought for higher endowments—superior illumination—knowlege, the poffeffion of which would put them on a footing of equality with the inhabitants of heaven. Instead of granting, God forbade them the thing they longed for. They obtained it under the agency of hell. By this disobedience, sin entered into the world, and death by sin. They gained corruption as an inheritance to themselves and their posterity. And though the Lord was so merciful that he forgave their misdeeds, and destroyed them not for ever, yet from this period their strength was only labour and sorrow; their wisdom was foolishness with God*.

* Gen. iii. 5, 8.

" Give

"Give me children, or I die," said the wife of the Patriarch. She had her requeſt; but it pleaſed God at the ſame moment to deſtroy her: and death went hand in hand with the boon ſhe had ſo paſſionately ſolicited *.

"Give us fleſh to eat," ſaid the people of Iſrael, in their paſſage through the wilderneſs. Though they were fed with Angels' food—though their heavenly Guide opened the rock of ſtone, and the waters flowed out, ſtill we find them on all occaſions lifting up their voices, not in praiſes, but in mutinous complaints againſt their Benefactor. "Our ſoul "loatheth this light bread—it were good "for us to be in Egypt!" The Author of nature heard, and he complied. An innumerable aſſemblage of winged fowls was brought to the deſert, to content their wayward appetite. "But, while the meat was yet in their mouths, the heavy

* Gen. xxx. 1.—xxxv. 19.

wrath of God came upon them, and flew the wealthiest of them, and smote down the choicest men that were in Israel*."

"Give us a king to reign over us!" Thus we find them exclaiming at a subsequent period, when, weary of the immediate sovereignty of their God, they clamorously demanded an earthly monarch. The divine Providence, justly irritated by their ingratitude, punished them with the severest of all punishments, the gratification of their desires. "He gave them a king in his anger;" not one whose virtues reflected lustre on the royal character—not a father of his people—not a dispenser of righteous judgement—not a faithful minister and vicegerent of God; but a king, calculated to make them feel the folly and impiety of their wishes—a bloody, remorseless, sacrilegious tyrant†.

* Numb. xi. 4.—Psal. lxxviii. 30, 31.
† 1 Sam. viii. 6.—xxii. 18, 19.

SERM.
VIII.
When the rebellious children of God had by more atrocious fins brought down on themfelves more grievous judgements—when the holy temple was deftroyed, and the devouring flames had laid wafte the hill of Sion—the remnant of Judah had a promife of deliverance and fafety, if they would fubmit to the protection of Heaven, and abandon the defign they had formed of efcaping into Egypt. At the fame moment the voice of God, by his prophet, denounced the utmoft feverity of the divine indignation, if they perfifted in their rafh and impious project. "Go ye not," faith he, "into "Egypt! Know certainly that ye fhall "die by the fword, by the famine, and "by the peftilence, in the place whither "ye defire to go, and to fojourn*." They went, and they returned no more.

We have no need, however, to multiply inftances from ancient times, when the cafe may now be brought home to every

* Jer. xli. 17.—xlii. 22.

one of us. Let us rather confider the tendency of thofe wifhes we are ourfelves fo anxious to frame.

The firft and moft general of thefe objects of defire is *Affluence*—partly from pride, and a fpirit of luxury; partly from a wifh to be independent on the Providence of God. We would fain be out of the reach of adverfity. But what faith the Scripture? " Woe to him that " coveteth an evil covetoufnefs to his " houfe, that he may fet his neft on " high, that he may be delivered from " the power of evil!" Alas, is there no evil but poverty to be dreaded? Will riches tend to make us wifer or better, or more fitted for heaven? will they prolong our lives, or remove our cares? Far, very far otherwife. The fleep of a labouring man is fweet, whether he eat little or much; but the abundance of the rich will not fuffer him to fleep. Indifference to the pure and innocent enjoy-

enjoyments of life, a wearisome pursuit of fugitive pleasures, a body palled by satiety, a mind over-worn with anxious solicitude, these, and such as these, are the common attendants on abundant wealth. "When goods increase, they are increased that eat them; and what good have the owners thereof, save the beholding them with their eyes?"

Power, and pre-eminence in rank, stand next in order among the gorgeous trifles of this world. Often do we find the whole soul of man, that soul, formed for the contemplation of eternity, and capable of holding converse with God, in a state of vassalage to the tyranny of pride.—But we proceed no further in this beaten path, so frequently trodden by them who have had occasion to investigate the passions and propensities of our nature. They have clearly, they have successfully demonstrated, that we cannot

not with any certainty judge for ourselves, what will be most conducive to our welfare. Neither riches, nor power, nor long life, nor a multitude of children, nor beauty, nor eloquence, nor shining talents, nor distinctions of any kind, can of themselves impart solid and substantial happiness. All things are in the hands of Him, who ordereth the events of our lives, not so much with a view to our immediate gratification as to our real benefit—and who knoweth, better than his fallible creatures, the things which belong to their present as well as their everlasting peace.

Now it is this all-perfect knowledge on the part of God, contrasted with the ignorance of man, which proves the folly and infatuation of our unqualified petitions to heaven. The objects of our wishes may be pernicious in themselves— they may be pernicious as far as concerns

SERM. VIII.

cerns us—or they may, although they appear to be intrinsically good, become the occasion of future and unsuspected evil. In these cases, the mercy of God consists, not in *granting*, but in *refusing*, the thing which we long for. The very disappointment, which may seem to us so grievous, is the effect of his fatherly goodness. A parent, anxious for his child, guards against his obtaining what may be prejudicial to him, though he desire it never so ardently. It is an act of cold indifference to acquiesce, where such acquiescence may be attended with danger. It is frequently in heavy displeasure, as we see abundantly exemplified in the sacred writings, that God consents to the wayward and imprudent wishes of man. " My people would not hear my voice, and Israel would not obey me, so I gave them up to their own hearts' lusts, and let them follow their own imaginations."

It

It would certainly demonstrate our prudence, and it would conduce to our happiness in the highest degree, if in cases where our wishes are frustrated, we were calmly and dispassionately to consider, whether we have any just cause of complaint? whether the wisdom of God hath not in view for us essential good, amidst all this seeming evil? whether we are competent judges of what is for our ultimate benefit, or of the steps that may lead to it? whether we are capable of ascertaining what is good for us, even in this life, which we spend as a shadow? But vain man would be wise—the primæval cause of his misery still pursues him—vain man would be wiser than his God. Grant me my request, though it destroy me! Give me the thing that I long for, though in the day that I taste thereof, I should surely die!

Are we then to make no request to the Almighty? Are we not, at the entrance and

and at the clofe of every day, to offer up our petitions to the throne of grace? Yes, verily: and He, through whofe merits our prayers are accepted, hath taught us how to pray. By that divine model let us regulate our addreffes to heaven. Without obftinately fixing on any determinate objects of anxious folicitation, let us refign ourfelves implicitly to our God. Let us pray, that, of his unbounded mercy, he would beftow on us what he knows to be moft for our benefit, not merely as inhabitants of this world, but as candidates for the glories of a better—that he would difpofe our hearts to contentment and patient refignation—that in cafes where our hopes are difappointed of their object, he would enable us to fay, with our ever bleffed-Saviour, " Not my will, O Father, but thine, be done"—that he would grant to us fuch a meafure of earthly comforts as may enable us to pafs in peace and innocence through this fleeting and tranfitory world;

world; but that, above all, he would prepare us for the enjoyment of permanent happiness, at his own time, in his heavenly kingdom. Thither let us aspire with all the ambition of which we are capable. On this subject we cannot form too ardent wishes, we cannot offer too importunate requests. If we ask in faith, nothing wavering, God will not cast out our prayers, nor turn his mercy from us.

Whenever therefore the tumultuous waves of adversity rage and swell against us, or whenever we are tempted, in the hour of prosperity, to form visionary hopes that ought not to be realised, then let us give more especial diligence to bring into subjection every thought to h e obedience of Christ. Then let us retire from the world—from its terrors, and from its allurements—and, in the language of solemn devotion, thus pour out our souls before our Father who seeth in secret:

"*O that*

SERM.
VIII.
"O *that I might have my request, and that God would grant me the thing that I long for;*
"*Even that it would please* God *to preserve and* save *me, through his mercy in* Jesus Christ *our Lord!* Amen."

SERMON IX.

THE JUST JUDGMENTS OF GOD.

SERMON

SERMON IX.

THE JUST JUDGMENTS OF GOD.

1 KINGS xxi.—29.

"*Seeſt thou, how Ahab humbleth himſelf before me? Becauſe he humbleth himſelf before me, I will not bring the evil in his days, but in his ſon's days will I bring the evil upon his houſe.*"

THAT it is lawful for the Almighty to do what he will with his own—that the God of all fleſh hath an abſolute and unlimited power over the creatures which

SERM. IX.

which he hath made—that, as we all have sinned, the divine Justice would have been only fulfilled, were every one of us to have perished without recovery—these are solemn and momentous truths, interwoven with the fundamental principles of our holy religion.

But, to our everlasting comfort, we are assured, that where Justice, abstracted from redeeming mercy, could not have failed to punish, the love of God in Christ interposed, and obliterated the sentence of death. Henceforth there is no condemnation to them that are in Christ Jesus; but, upon our true contrition and penitence, through his merits, and the satisfaction of his precious blood, we are saved from the wrath to come. So that, under the gospel-covenant of propitiation, we can sing both of mercy and judgment unto the Lord, and celebrate each of these divine attributes, as operating jointly for our everlasting benefit.

Thus

Thus much I conceived it abſolutely neceſſary to premiſe, as the foundation of thoſe arguments which I ſhall offer on a point, where often through mortal weakneſs, and ſtill oftener through mortal preſumption, the juſtice of the Almighty has been moſt raſhly and indecently queſtioned. "Suffer me a little, and I will ſhew you that I have to ſpeak in God's behalf."

But let me, at the ſame moment, diſclaim all idea, that the divine procedure towards mankind does of itſelf ſtand in need of vindication. "He is a Rock, his work is perfect; for all his ways are judgement, a God of truth, and without iniquity, juſt and right is He." Yet, while the ungodly mocketh at the counſel of God, and while they that are unlearned and unſtable wreſt ſuch things as are hard to be underſtood to their own deſtruction, it is the earneſt deſire of my heart to throw ſome light on a very obſcure and myſterious ſubject:

The *juſt Judgments of God.*

SERM. IX.

ſubject: to remove any doubt that may have ariſen in the minds of thoſe who hear me: to "aſſert eternal Pro-
"vidence, and juſtify the ways of God
"to man."

You have not perhaps found it eaſy to reconcile the words of my text with thoſe notions which you would wiſh to entertain of that gracious and merciful Being who is over all, God bleſſed for ever.

AHAB, king of Iſrael, having incurred the diſpleaſure of Heaven by many and grievous offences, and having in a flagrant inſtance cruelly ſeized on poſſeſſions which had been purchaſed at the price of innocent blood, was met by the prophet of God with awful denunciations of evil. Penetrated with ſhame and remorſe, Ahab ſought to make atonement for his ſin, by every token of ſincere and heart-felt repentance. HE who deſpiſeth

not

not the fighing of a contrite heart, looked with an eye of favour on his fuppliant: and a voice from Heaven addreffed Elijah in thefe remarkable words: " Seeft thou, how Ahab humbleth " himfelf before me? becaufe he hum- " bleth himfelf before me, I will not " bring the evil in his days; *but in his* " *fon's days will I bring the evil upon his* " *houfe.*"

Thus the cafe ftands in the particular inftance we are this day to confider: to explin away which, if poffible, would be of no avail, as the divine affertions in the fecond commandment and elfewhere would ftill ftand in full force, " that God vifiteth the iniquity of the fathers upon the children, unto the third and fourth generation."

I would therefore earneftly folicit your attention to the two following remarks, which ftand fupported by undeniable proof from holy fcripture, and which, when

when admitted, will obviate all the difficulties that, on firſt inſpection, ſeem to overſhadow the ſubject.

The firſt is this, *That theſe judgments, which are recorded as inflicted by God on the children, for the ſake of their parents' ſins, are conſtantly, and without any exception, judgments of a* temporal, *and not of a* ſpiritual *nature.*

Nothing therefore is by any means implied, which tends to overthrow the aſſertion of the prophet, "The soul " that ſinneth, it ſhall die. The ſon " ſhall not bear the iniquity of the fa- " ther, neither ſhall the father bear " the iniquity of the ſon : the righteouſ- " neſs of the righteous ſhall be upon him, " and the wickedneſs of the wicked " ſhall be upon him." Still doth the word of God ſtand ſure—as will be fully manifeſted in the great Day of retribution, when the ſecrets of all hearts ſhall be revealed, and every man ſhall receive

a juſt

a juft recompence for that he hath done, whether it be good, or bad.

The fecond obfervation I would make is, *That even thefe temporal judgements, denounced againft the children of difobedient parents, have very rarely been inflicted, where the parties have fhewn any difpofition to avert the impending fentence, and to feek the favour of that God, whom their fathers provoked by their abominations.*

So that the denunciation of punifhment being that of punifhment merely temporal, and even this for the moft part remiffible, (if the children have not walked in the way of their forefathers, but have done that which is right in the fight of the Lord), the mercy of our compaffionate and tender Father appears in all its luftre, notwithftanding it hath been moft unworthily and impioufly queftioned in the prefent inftance, as in many others, when mortal man would be be more juſt than God, when a human creature would be more pure than his Creator.

To theſe two remarks allow me to add a third, of a ſtill more extenſive nature—*That all the forewarnings of vengeance in the ſacred writings, againſt thoſe who had actually offended, do neceſſarily imply, that the perſons ſo threatened* continue *in their ſin.* The predicted evil is not carried into execution, if the wicked man turn away from the wickedneſs he hath committed, and do that which is lawful and right. Not that the decrees of God are thereby fruſtrated, or that the word which proceeded out of his lips is rendered of none effect; for the expreſs object of the divine threatening was, that the ſinner might fear, and amend. "It may be," ſaith the Lord to Jeremiah, "it may be, "that the houſe of Judah will hear all "the evil that I purpoſe to do unto "them, that they may return every man "from

The just Judgments of God.

" from his evil way, *that I may forgive their transgression and their sin.*" To this we may add the memorable expostulation in Ezekiel: " Have I any pleasure at all in the death of him that dieth, saith the Lord God; and not that he should return from his ways, and live? Cast away from you all your transgressions, and make you a new heart, and a new spirit; for why will ye die, O house of Israel?"

If there be any who *doubt* the assertion, that the punishments spoken of as inflicted on children for the sins of their parents are merely of a temporal nature, let me intreat them to weigh well in their minds that dreadful conclusion which results from the contrary opinion— It is no other than this: " That a just, and holy, and merciful God dooms an immortal soul to irreversible destruction, on account of offences in which that soul had no share whatever!" An inference

rence of such a nature, as to make us tremble, while we speak or hear it—and which yet cannot be done away, unless the position we have laid down is admitted in its full force.

But what it is blasphemy even to conceive with respect to the souls of those, who are threatened for the offences of their parents, we may very safely adopt as to their bodies, their lives, or fortunes. It may have very highly promoted the cause of truth and holiness, that some marked instances of the vengeance of God against sin should have been displayed even against the posterity of the sinner, that others, admonished by such examples, might, for their childrens' sake, if not for their own, take heed how they offended. Add to this, that the Almighty hath it in his power to make such ample recompence in heaven to those, who are tried in the furnace of adversity upon earth—the eternal weight of of glory fo overbalances the light afflictions which endure for a moment, that if, in thefe few and evil days, (which are but as a little moment when compared with the ages of eternity) the finner's defcendant fhould be vifited by the divine correction, he will have no caufe to murmur at the difpenfations of the Almighty, if, after he hath been a little chaftifed, he be greatly rewarded. For who fhall fay, that thefe very afflictions, if they were properly received, were not of themfelves the guides to happinefs—efpecially where an erroneous education and evil example had probably hardened the feelings againft the common means of grace and falvation?

The divine judgements were denounced againft the family of Ahab; and his numerous progeny actually fell by the fword. But let us not doubt, that if among them there was one, who by his regard

SERM.
IX.
regard to the laws of God had any claim to heavenly mercy, let us not doubt that he received the end of his faith, even the falvation of his foul. We have the divine authority for faying, that the fon of the wicked Jeroboam found favour with God—and yet that young prince was then actually expiring in the flower of his age, and was foon followed, with tears and lamentations, to an untimely grave. Early death is by no means fent as an indication of the difpleafure of God to thofe whom he may call to himfelf, however grievous the punifhment may be to the defolate furvivors. Many, as far as themfelves are concerned, having lived a fhort time, fulfil a long time. Wifdom is as the grey hair unto men, and unfpotted life is as old age. Jofiah himfelf, the beloved of God, was involved in the doom pronounced againft the family of the impious Manaffes, and perifhed, in the meridian of life, by the fword of the Egyptian tyrant.

We

We are, secondly, to confider, that thefe inflictions of vicarious punifhment very unfrequently occur: never, indeed, but under circumftances of extreme atrocity. *National* impiety has, for the moft part, given rife to them, when the goodnefs, and forbearance, and long-fuffering of God has been rafhly and fatally defpifed. But, as we have already obferved, even with refpect to temporal afflictions, the divine mercy hath been pleafed in many cafes to remit the fentence, when they, againft whom the threatening was prounonced, have (through prayer and timely repentance) fought earneftly for the favour of God.

One painful and melancholy confideration, however, fuggefts itfelf to the mind. That the children of ungodly parents have themfelves been too generally difpofed to *increafe*, rather than to *leffen*, the weight of divine indignation: and, inftead of imploring the Almighty to ftay his hand

hand from smiting them, have, by their misconduct, obstructed all the avenues of heavenly mercy, and brought down twofold vengeance on their own heads.

Can the most heedless parent endure a reflection like this? Can he endure the thought, that his daring impiety—his violation of the laws of God, will too probably teach his unhappy children to become transgressors like himself, and to rush precipitately into the abyss of destruction?—so that it had been good for them never to have been born into the world, or to have been called from it in their earliest infancy, before they became familiarized to sin?

It is, indeed, a difficult task for those who have been brought up under the guidance of the wicked, to abstain from following the evil example constantly before their eyes. We read, that " Ahaziah the son " of Ahab did evil in the sight of the " Lord—

"Lord—that he walked in the way of "his father, and in the way of his mo- "ther, and in the way of Jeroboam the "son of Nebat; who made Ifrael to fin— "that he ferved Baal, and worſhipped "him; and provoked to anger the Lord "God of Ifrael, *according to all that his* "*father had done.*" His unhappy brother alſo, who, after the death of Ahaziah, fate upon the throne of Ifrael, feared not to fin againſt the Almighty by abominable idolatries. The fons of Ahab were perfecutors, tyrants, and murderers *. They did not deprecate the wrath of God— they did not humble themſelves under his mighty hand—they added rebellion unto fin, and multiplied their offences againſt the Almighty. Can we wonder then that they " were confumed in their " own wickednefs?" that the threatened vengeance fell in thunders on their guilty

---

* The expreſſion of Eliſha concerning Jehoram is very remarkable. He is called בן הרצחה *Filius* Sicarii, 2 Kings vi. 32.

SERM. IX.

heads? that, provoked by their repeated enormities, the Almighty stretched out the arm of his indignation, and destroyed them from off the face of the earth?

I come now to the third particular offered to your consideration at the commencement of this discourse; and, lo, a cloud of witnesses arise to confirm and illustrate the assertion. I mean, that all the forewarnings of judgments in Scripture, however absolutely worded, imply *continuance in sin* in the parties against whom such vengeance was denounced. Thus God, speaking by his prophet Isaiah, tells his people, that, when they stretched forth their hands, he would hide his eyes from them: when they made many prayers, he would not hear. The reason is given—Their hands were defiled with blood. But mark what immediately follows. " Wash ye, make you clean; put away the evil of your doings from before mine eyes; cease to do evil, learn to do well. Then though your sins be as scarlet, they shall be white as snow—though they be red like crimson, they shall be as wool!"

Hear the testimony of the holy prophet Daniel, when called on to explain to Nebuchadnezzar his mysterious dream. "They shall drive thee, O King, from men, and thy dwelling shall be with the beasts of the field, till thou shalt know that the heavens do rule. Wherefore, O King Nebuchadnezzar, let my counsel be acceptable unto thee; and break off thy sins by righteousness, and thine iniquities by shewing mercy to the poor; *if it may be a lengthening of thy tranquillity.*"

What could be more positive than the threatenings against the antient Jerusalem? Yet we find, that in the very moment of its fall, obedience on the part of Zedekiah would have arrested the

the impending blow, and saved an otherwise devoted city. "Thus saith the Lord, the God of hosts, the God of Israel—If thou wilt assuredly go forth unto the King of Babylon's princes, then thy soul shall live, and this city shall not be burnt with fire—Obey, I beseech thee, the voice of the Lord which I speak unto thee; so shall it be well unto thee, and thy soul shall live." But the infatuated King, and his obdurate people, were equally deaf to conviction; and the predicted ruin took its course.

"YET FORTY DAYS, AND NINEVEH SHALL BE OVERTHROWN." How express the tremendous declaration! But the people believed God, and they cried mightily unto him—they turned every one from his evil way, and from the violence that was in their hands. And God saw their works, that they turned from their evil way, and God repented of of the evil that he said he would do unto them, and he did it not.

Thus we see, that, whether with respect to a nation, or a man only, God is justified when he speaketh, and clear when he judgeth. Who shall not tremble at his justice? who shall not bless and adore his mercy?

I shall sum up what has been said in the memorable words of Elihu*:

"Hearken unto me, ye men of under-
"standing. Far be it from God, that he
"should do wickedness, and from the
"Almighty, that he should commit ini-
"quity. For the work of a man shall he
"render unto him, and cause every man
"to find according to his ways. Yea,
"surely, God will not do iniquity—nor
"will the Almighty pervert judgment.

* Job xxxiv. 10, 11, 12, 21, 23, 19.

"For his eyes are upon the fons of men, and he feeth all their goings. He will not lay upon men more than is right— for they are all the work of his hands."

Now to Father, Son, and Holy Ghoſt, the God of truth, of juſtice, of holineſs, of mercy, whoſe ways are not as our ways, nor whoſe thoughts as our thoughts, be aſcribed, as is moſt due, all honour, power, might, majeſty, and dominion, now and for evermore. Amen.

SERMON X.

THE CLOSE OF THE YEAR.

SERMON X.

THE CLOSE OF THE YEAR.

ISAIAH lxiv. 6.

We all do fade as a leaf.

THE silent lapse of time has imperceptibly led us onwards, and another year is departing, to return no more. It is a moment which calls for serious and solemn meditation. Various, and often-repeated, are the lessons which teach us the true condition of our nature: " Day " after day uttereth speech, and night " after night sheweth knowlege." Either

ther we are admonished by some melancholy example of mortality—or we are warned in our own persons by pain and sickness—or we observe the visible effects which revolving hours produce in others—or, at all events, the expiration of one of these portions of time into which our lives are divided, compels us to form a just estimate of our fleeting existence; and to confess, that when a few days are come, then we shall go the way whence we shall not return.

My brethren, if you come hither prompted by Athenian curiosity, and desiring to hear *some new thing* *, you entertain a wish, which, on the present occasion, cannot be gratified. I speak that you do know; and testify that, to which the events of every year bear witness. Can novelty be expected in a discourse

* See Acts xvii. 21.

on the frailty and precariousness of our being?

Man is like a thing of nought—his time passeth away like a shadow. It is fitting, therefore, that we mark the gradations towards eternity, and fortify ourselves, by previous exercise and discipline, for that solemn event which is ordained for all the children of men. Let the momentous truth be ever present to our minds, that *we all do fade as a leaf*. Considerations of this nature will, by the grace of God, " turn highly to our profit, and help us forward in the right way, that leadeth to everlasting life."

Let us meditate on these things—let us give ourselves wholly to them—let us write them on the tablet of our hearts.

But, before we proceed in our enquiry, let us pause, and make a short retrospect.

SERM. spect. Let the various events of the now-
X. concluding year pass in review before
our eyes—the mercies and deliverances
vouchsafed to us—the interpositions of
Providence in our favour—the blessings
we have enjoyed—the sorrows we have
sustained—the warnings we have received.
Who among the sons of men, after
considering the past days of his life, will
not confess, from his own personal experience,
that the goodness of God endureth continually?

That we live—that we breathe—that
we are in possession of our intellectual
powers—these in themselves afford abundant
cause of thankfulness. That the
earth brings forth in profusion whatever
is necessary for our sustenance or enjoyment—that
an unseen hand administers
to us our daily bread—that we have rain
from heaven, and fruitful seasons—these
are thy bounteous gifts, O Lord! and
they demand from thine adoring creatures

tures the tribute of univerfal praife. What are our pretenfions to thy favour? What works of righteoufnefs have we done, that we fhould receive fuch inceffant tokens of thy parental love?

The cup of human life, however, cannot long remain unmixed with forrow. Some of thofe who hear me, have poffibly tafted its bitter ingredients, even to the dregs. They have fuftained the preffure of adverfity; they have experienced the acute or lingering pains of ficknefs; or, what is yet more grievous, they have feen the ftroke of death inflicted on fome much-loved friend, in whofe fociety all their earthly delights centered, and without whom the world is but as a defolate wildernefs. To fuch mourners as thefe, where we fpeak of the fhortnefs of this tranfitory life, we hold out no confideration of terror—rather do we adminifter a lenient balm, and mitigate the anguifh of the troubled foul.

SERM. X.

Arise from the earth, O thou that art afflicted, and lift up thine head; sorrow not for the departed, as if thou wert without hope. They have but preceded thee in the path of immortality: thou shalt go to them, but they shall not return to thee.

While we contemplate the procedure of God towards us, it is highly expedient that we reflect likewise on our own actions, and ask ourselves, in what manner we have fulfilled the important obligations we owe to our God. And this is an enquiry not to be entered upon lightly, and without consideration. It demands the best energies of our souls. It is a question in which our eternal salvation is immediately involved.

Let us review therefore, with impartial judgment, the various sins and offences of our lives.

How

How many duties have been left unperformed! How many Sabbaths have been profaned! How many opportunities of partaking the Holy Communion have been neglected! How many distressed sufferers have been dismissed without relief! How many calls of the divine grace have been unthankfully disregarded! How many admonitions of a merciful Providence have been suffered to pass by unheeded! Or, further, how many sad and grievous sins have been actually committed, either to the scandal of society, or in a manner only less shameful, because more secret! If God were extreme to mark what is done amiss, who among the children of men should abide the dreadful sentence? But there is mercy with him; and the best of us have abundant need for the exercise of that mercy. We must beware, however, that we trifle not with the heavenly gift, lest it should be for ever withdrawn from us—lest we should feel the just indignation

tion of Him whom we have prefumptuoufly dared to offend. Swift is the courfe of thofe hours which are leading us to the grave. Frail and precarious are the moments of our exiftence. Teach thy fervants, O God, fo to number their days, that they may apply their hearts unto that wifdom which is from above. Teach them, that although they have done iniquity, yet, if they repent, and fin no more, then, through the merits of their divine Interceffor, they fhall live—they fhall not die. Teach them, that this tranfient fcene is melting away like a fhadow from before their eyes, and that the kingdom of heaven is at hand. But, above all, teach them, that, when the breath of man goeth forth, when he returns to his earth, and when all his thoughts, as far as concern mortality, fhall perifh, then bleffed, and only bleffed is he, " who hath the God of Jacob for his help, and whofe hope is in the Lord his God."

The comparison between human and vegetable life has been elegantly descanted on by authors of the earliest antiquity—it has been stated, with eloquence and precision, by divines and moralists of later times—but more particularly we find it illustrated, by all the varieties of metaphor, throughout the figurative language of holy scripture. And surely no comparison can be more apposite, no similitude more affectingly obvious.

When you hear of infancy sent to an early grave—when you behold youth and beauty languishing under deadly sickness, does not the image force itself on your minds of a fair and blooming flower, suddenly cut down by the pitiless hand of the destroyer? Or look around you—the world is now wintry; those leaves which so lately flourished in all the perfection of their richest verdure, now lie scattered upon the ground, faded,

faded, lifeless, discoloured, and about to mingle with their parent earth! Let us read our destiny in theirs—from the dust we likewise had our origin, and thither we likewise shall return.

The parallel so accurately drawn in my text, in its primary signification, adapts itself to the natural decay of age, as typified by the falling of the *withered* leaf. But is it not also strictly applicable to the termination of our existence at other periods? Are there not storms and tempests, which, even in the midst of summer, deprive the trees of their luxuriant foliage, and lay prostrate on the ground the glory of the once-smiling year? Is there not the slow-consuming canker? is there not the devouring worm, that prematurely destroys while yet in the bloom, or even in the bud, the hope and the pride of spring? We are more than justified in the application of the fading leaf to death, come

as

as it will, at any time, or in any form. At whatever feafon our life is brought to its conclufion we do moſt aſſuredly fade as the leaf, all of us.

And here I cannot but mention, as a circumſtance immediately connected with my prefent fubject, the wonderful fimilarity which fubfifts betwixt the mechanifm of the human frame and the fyſtem of vegetation. More particularly in the conſtruction of a leaf (the fymbol of our tranfitory nature), the eye of philofophy fees an infinite variety of nerves, fibres, ligaments—pores innumerable—veſſels which convey to thofe pores perfpirable juices for their difcharge—a fluid which preferves life throughout all the delicate contexture, and even a circulation of that fluid, correfpondent to that of the blood in organic living bodies. But I muſt not indulge myfelf in carrying into length a fubject rather curious than ufeful, any further

SERM. X. further than as it teaches us to adore the Creator in his marvellous works, the refult of confummate wifdom, and of divine Omnipotence.

"All flefh is grafs," faith our prophet, "and all the goodlinefs thereof "as the flower of the field." We have feen that this is the cafe in its phyfical fenfe; let us proceed to examine its moral application.

We, like the plants and flowers, have our fpring, which ufhers us into life, when we burft forth in all the luxuriance of early beauty. The fummer, the high meridian of our days, next advances, when we flourifh in the full maturity of ftrength and comelinefs. Before we are confcious of the alteration, but probably not before others have perceived it, the blooming tints of youth, the ripened graces of manhood are gradually

retiring

retiring from us, and we fall into our autumnal wane. One more change awaits us, and completes the revolution of our days. Soon, very foon, are we led on by the withering hand of old age to the winter of death. And lo, when we are paſſed away, another generation cometh in our place, to whom life is imparted on conditions exactly fimilar to thoſe ordained to us when we entered on our portion of exiſtence. In like manner, when the winter of nature is paſt, a freſh fucceſſion of leaves will appear, and will flouriſh during their appointed feafon—God reneweth the face of the earth—another and another progeny will follow—and, as long as the world endureth, one event happeneth unto all. *" All fleſh waxeth old as a garment ; and the covenant from the beginning is, Thou ſhalt die the death. As of the green leaves on a thick tree, fome fall and fome grow ; ſo is the generation of fleſh*

SERM.
X.
and blood: one cometh to an end, and another is born *."

If thefe things are fo (and infidelity itfelf dares not gainfay them) is it not our intereft, as well as our duty, to improve diligently that portion of time which is allotted to us? Ought we not, with unremitting earneftnefs, to work out our own falvation while it is yet day—while it pleafes God to continue to us our precarious being? O let us be wife—let us underftand this—let us confider our approaching end! Let us not fail to remember, that there is a period, at which the parallel betwixt the rational and vegetable world ceafes, and holds good no longer. We fade, it is true, like the leaf; but *we* do not perifh in utter annihilation. That folemn hour, in which we fhall be called from the bofom of the earth, that folemn hour will bear witnefs to the great, the momentous difference. Then our cor-

* Ecclefiafticus xiv. 17, 18:

ruptible

ruptible body shall put on incorruption, and shall be reanimated by that immortal spirit, which was infused into man by the breath of God, when he made him " in the image of his own eternity." Then they who sleep in Christ shall arise from the dark recesses of the grave to the liberty and light of heaven. They shall rejoice with joy unspeakable and full of glory. From the desolate and dreary mansions of the tomb they shall pass to their better country; they shall be planted in the house of the Lord; they shall flourish in the courts of the house of their God.

The conviction, that we are so much nearer to our death, presses on us with irresistible force, at the conclusion of each passing year. It challenges, it commands our attention. Those in particular, who are far advanced on the journey of life, must be callous and insensible indeed, if they neglect the great duty of

prepa-

SERM. X. preparation. Speedily muft that hour arrive, in which they will be fummoned to join the number of departed fpirits, at His command, "in whofe hand is the foul of all men living, and the breath of all mankind." But is the warning voice alone directed to the aged and full of days? Is man, at any period, in a ftate of fecurity? Can mortals be fo prefumptuous as to rely on the long continuance of their exiftence, becaufe they are in the enjoyment of youth, and health, and vigour? Thofe poffeffions of which we can in one moment be deprived, ought not to be trufted in for one moment. We dwell in houfes of clay. Be the ftructure ever fo beautiful, ever fo apparently fecure, ftill its foundation is in the duft. Boaft not thyfelf then, O vain man—boaft not thyfelf in thy tranfitory glory; for thou knoweft not what a day may bring forth.

Marvel

Marvel not, my beloved brethren, at this train of awful ideas. To every thing there is a season, and a time to every purpose under heaven. This is the time for solemn reflection. Godly sorrow worketh life: Godly seriousness produces effects which are likewise in their proportion beneficial. When the time of our departure is at hand, we shall not regret that we have employed some of our better hours in meditating on, and preparing for, its approach. Blessed is that servant, whom his Lord, when he cometh, shall find watching.

What if thoughts of this nature tend to banish levity and senseless mirth? Be it so. "The heart is made better*." The faithful believer feels no sensations of horror, when he reflects that we all do fade as the leaf. That melancholy which the idea of dissolution spreads over his mind is sweetly corrected and softened

* Ecclesiastes vii. 3.

SERM. X. softened down by the blessed hope of everlasting life, which he claims as his inheritance through the Saviour, the Lord Jesus Christ. Of this hope nothing can deprive him. Neither age, nor infirmity, nor sickness, nor pain, nor poverty, nor distress, nor the treachery of friends, nor the fury of enemies, nor the scorn of men, nor the malice of devils, nor death itself, nor the gates of hell, can finally prevail against it.

Happy are they, who, while they sojourn in this valley of tears, are thus visited by the Day-spring from on high. The troubles and vicissitudes of this perishable world are considered by them as preparatory to an immutable state of felicity and glory. He, in whom they believed, shall be their guide even unto death, " Jesus Christ, the same yesterday, " and to-day, and for ever." Though they flee away as the shadow that departeth—though they are cut off from the

the land of the living, yet is their hope full of immortality. Though their outward man perish, yet their inward man is renewed day by day. "The grafs "withereth, the flower fadeth, but the "word of the Lord endureth for ever." The Author of eternal life will keep them safe who are committed to his truft. They are the children of God, even the children of the refurrection.

In full affurance of faith, let us lift up our eyes to the everlafting kingdom of our Father. In that kingdom is the throne of his majefty eftablifhed, and there it remaineth from generation to generation. There, All-Great, All-Perfect, All-Bleffed, he reigneth over heaven and earth, difpofing at his pleafure of the whole creation. There, in the effulgence of a light to which the mortal thought cannot approach, he receiveth the homage of all the celeftial celestial powers, and hears the wonders of his praise uttered by the voices of innumerable angels. Before him, in the mystery of the ever-blessed Trinity, all the host of heaven cast their crowns in humble adoration, saying, " Hallelu" jah—salvation to Him that sitteth upon " the throne, and to the Lamb! Bless" ing, and honour, and glory, and pow" er, be unto him that sitteth upon the " throne for ever and ever. Holy, holy, " holy, Lord God Almighty, which art, " and which wast, and which art to " come! Heaven and earth are full of " the majesty of thy glory. Through " the countless ages of eternity THOU " ART THE SAME, AND THY YEARS SHALL " NOT FAIL."

SERMON XI.

THE NATURE OF CHRISTIAN FAITH.

SERMON

SERMON XI.

THE NATURE OF CHRISTIAN FAITH.

HEBREWS xi.—1.

Now faith is the substance of things hoped for, the evidence of things not seen.

SUCH is the definition which the Holy Spirit hath left on record of the best and most precious of his heavenly gifts[*]. Glorious is the scene exhibited in the subsequent recital, when we behold the martyrs and heroes of religion, rising as

[*] See 1 Cor. xii. 9.

SERM.
XI.
it were from their state of hallowed rest, and passing along, in bright succession, before our eyes. With joy unspeakable we see them exhibiting the illustrious trophies of faith, and triumphing, because of the truth. Under the banner of faith they went undaunted to the conflict, through the allpowerful succour of faith they obtained the victory. Now are they numbered among the children of God, and their names are in the book of life.

Blessed be the God and Father of our Lord Jesus Christ, who hath begotten us to a lively hope by the same allpowerful evidence, which is to us also the foretaste and the earnest of our promised inheritance. That light, which once shined on the saints of old, even now diffuseth its blessed influence upon us. Even now it is a guide to our feet, and a lamp unto our paths.

Would

Would you contemplate the perfect work of faith? Behold the true Believer in the hour of his sorrow. Behold him, rising superior to those dreadful trials of his constancy, which it should seem impossible for his nature to support. He endures affliction and pain in all its horrible varieties. He suffers and he dies with patient serenity, looking unto Jesus, the author and finisher of his faith. Through life, and in death, the operation of faith on the soul of man produces joy, and comfort, and patience, where without this blessed principle all would be sorrow, perturbation, and despair. It charms to rest those torturing passions, which otherwise would rage with incessant fury; and, by suggesting the rewards of an eternal state, bears us through all the struggles and temptations, and calamities attendant on this miserable world. "Fear thou not," a voice seems to say, "for He is with thee—" be not dismayed, for he is thy God—
" he

SERM.
XI.
" he will ſtrengthen thee, yea, he will
" help thee, yea, he will uphold thee
" with the arm of his righteouſneſs."

Let us then, my brethren, contemplate more fully the beneficial effects of our chriſtian faith: how, by being the ſubſtance of things hoped for, it keeps alive the chearing influence of hope in our minds—how, by being the evidence of things as yet unſeen, it gives us ſuch a proſpect of future glory, as to render us triumphant and victorious over preſent miſery. Let us ſee how it accompanies us in our pilgrimage towards a better country—how it guides us in difficulties, comforts us in all trouble, mitigates the pains of death, and opens the gate of heaven.

The firſt conſideration, which preſents itſelf to our minds on this exalted ſubject, is, that the bleſſings and privileges attendant on faith are peculiar to Chriſtianity.

tianity. No other system (the law excepted which was to lead us to Christ), no other system whatever held out those pure and perfect objects, on which alone the soul can assuredly rest. The heathens knew it not. Those lettered sages, to whom we look up with astonishment, admiring their brilliant attainments, and the vast powers of their minds, were, on this first and greatest question, in the delusions of ignorance and error—while to their honour be it remembered, that the faint and imperfect glimmerings of light, which long-enfeebled tradition afforded them, were cherished with peculiar care—that they clung, with enthusiastic fondness, to the possibility of that future unseen state, whereof they were in possession of no certain evidence—that they grasped at the shadow of things hoped for, because they had not the substance.

SERM. XI.

It is to the exclusive praise of the religion of Christ Jesus, that it inculcates in all their perfection those doctrines, the belief of which constitutes "the life of God in the soul of man:" teaching us to see Him who is invisible; setting before us the Creation, Redemption, and Sanctification, of the world by GOD the Father, GOD the Son, and GOD the Holy Ghost; and preparing us for the final dissolution of the things which we now behold around us, and the restoration of our mortal body to the immortal spirit, after the hand of death shall for a time have parted them asunder.

Thus through faith we understand that the worlds were framed by the word of God, and that all the wonders of nature have their origin in His goodness and in His power. The Lord gave the word, and behold darkness was converted into light, confusion into order, deformity into symmetry and beauty. By his

excel-

excellent wifdom he made the heavens. He ſtretched out the dry land above the waters. He clad the earth with verdure, and brought forth all the treaſures of vegetation. He made great lights, and enriched the canopy of heaven with glittering ſtars. He cauſed the earth and the waters to bring forth abundantly the moving creature that had life, beaſts and all cattle, worms and feathered fowls. And GOD made man in His own image.

Through faith we underſtand, that man, thus created after the ſimilitude of God, is endowed with an immortal, incorruptible ſpirit ; which, though confined for a ſeaſon within the limits of a periſhable body, is in itſelf a portion of the divine eſſence myſteriouſly communicated from above. And further, that when this union between body and ſpirit ſhall be ſuſpended by death, the body ſhall return to earth as it was, but the

SERM. XI. the fpirit fhall return unto God who gave it.

Through faith we underftand that in the unfeen world, the expectation of which affords hope and comfort and a crown of rejoicing to the Believer, there are feparate manfions of joy and of forrow—where life eternal* will be the portion of all who have obeyed the commandments of their God; and everlafting punifhment* will overwhelm thofe who have tranfgreffed his laws, and violated his facred precepts.

But " all have finned, and come fhort of the glory of God." By the offence of our firft parents, and by our own actual frailty, we are all amenable to the dreadful fentence. Sin entered into the world, and death by fin. Now then, where is our hope? Through faith we underftand, that the only-be-

* Matt. xxv. 46.

gotten

gotten Son of God, our Lord Jesus Christ, taking upon him our flesh, became a willing and an all-sufficient sacrifice for the sins of the whole world—who, being the brightness of his Father's glory, and the express image of his person, did humble his soul unto death, made oblation and satisfaction for all our offences, and returned, a mighty Conqueror, to partake of that ineffable glory wherewith he was endued before the mountains were brought forth, and ever the earth and the world were made, being from everlasting to everlasting God of God and Lord of Lord*. As by one man's disobedience many were made sinners, even so by the obedience of one shall many be made righteous. Now then there is no condemnation for them that are in Christ Jesus, who walk not after the flesh, but after the spirit.

* See the note at p. 60.

This is the moſt ſublime and illuſtrious object of contemplation on which our faith can exerciſe itſelf; namely the Sun of Righteouſneſs, like the great luminary of heaven, pervading all the intellectual and ſpiritual ſyſtem, directing its various movements, inſpiring, illuminating, invigorating, animating the whole.

Through faith we underſtand and are ſure, that our mortal body, which ere long muſt periſh, and to all appearance be no more, will, at the laſt day, be again united to that immortal ſpirit, from which it hath for a while been ſeparated by death—that by the mighty power of God it ſhall be inveſted with new life, a life never more to be terminated. It ſhall be renewed after the likeneſs of our Creator and Redeemer, and mortality ſhall be ſwallowed up in glory.

Everlaſting

Everlasting happiness then is the ultimate object, the great and solemn completion of our faith. Faith leads us to the heaven of heavens. It points to our enraptured view the throne of God, and Jesus standing at the right-hand of God. It enables us to behold the transcendent glory of the Omnipotent—and while we contemplate the regions of bliss, illuminated by his presence, faith assures us of our future reception into the land of righteousness, the holy hill and heavenly kingdom; that eternal, incorruptible, unfading inheritance, reserved for the children of God. Conducted by this unerring guide, the Christian ascends from earth to heaven—from the shadow of death to the holy of holies; and he waits, in humble patience, for that welcome hour, when they who know their master now by faith, shall, after this life, have the fruition of his glorious Godhead.

These

SERM. XI.

These are the fruits produced in the regenerate soul by that substantial evident faith whereof we speak. From this pure source hath ever been derived that heroic constancy, which rendered the servants of God triumphant over tribulation, and torture, and ignominy, and death. They took pleasure in reproaches, in persecutions, in distresses—they were enabled to endure all things through Christ who strengthened them. The fiery darts of the wicked were repelled and quenched by the shield of faith. When enemies oppressed them they were not dismayed; they remembered that God was their shield, and the High God their Redeemer. This gave them light in darkness, joy in sorrow, comfort in the hour of tribulation. They called upon God, and were delivered; they put their trust in Him, and were not confounded. When they were in sickness or pain, they looked for relief to the great Physician of of souls—when they suffered poverty and the want of all things, they remembered Him who had not where to lay his head. When they were traduced and calumniated, they considered Him who endured such contradictions of sinners against himself. Always did they bear about in their body the dying of the Lord Jesus, that the life also of Jesus might be manifest in this body. When they mourned for others who were fallen asleep, they sorrowed not as those without hope; for, believing that Jesus died and rose again, they likewise believed and were sure, that those who were fallen asleep in Jesus, God would hereafter bring with him.

Such is the perfect work of christian faith, accompanied, as it must ever be, by christian hope. By the united efficacy of these inestimable gifts, we receive the promises, and we rejoice in the expectation of their accomplishment. We know,

SERM.
XI.
know, that Chrift is rifen from the dead. We know alfo, that he is the firft-fruits of an harveft, and that all the fheaves of the field fhall follow him. We behold him feated on the right hand of God. We are fully perfuaded, that he is gone to prepare a place for us. We believe, that he fhall return to judge the world. We are affured, that his reward is with him. That we may abound in hope through the power of the Holy Ghoft, the God of hope fills us with all joy and peace in believing—it follows therefore as a neceffary confequence, that where there is no faith, there can be no hope: and fuch as the world would be, without the light of the fun to gild and adorn the objects of creation, fuch is the life of man without the hope of Chriftianity *.

* For many of the fentiments, and fome of the expreffions in this difcourfe, the author is happy to confefs his obligations to the Reverend William Jones, A. M. minifter of Nayland.

To the unbeliever, all things are dark and gloomy—pleafure is worthlefs, and pain is infupportable. If at any time he is minifhed and brought low, through affliction, through pain, and trouble, he has no ftrong hold to flee unto from the preffure of his mifery. He will not feek unto God—unto God he will not commit his caufe—he faith in his heart " There " is no God"—he defpairs, and he dies. In the volume of the book of truth we have on record the hiftory of many perfons, who thus, abandoning the fuccours of religion and reafon, would not wait the appointed time till their change fhould come; but rufhed, with dreadful precipitancy, into the prefence of their God. And who were they? They were apoftates, infidels, traitors, parricides. The fierce and bloody Saul—the bafe Ahithophel—Zimri, who flew his mafter—and that " fon of perdition," who betrayed the innocent Jefus into the hands

SERM. XI.

hands of his implacable enemies. Satan is a murderer from the beginning : his delight is in the defperation of thofe who rafhly abandon themfelves to his pernicious guidance : he cometh but to kill and to deftroy. On the contrary, it is the office of the Meffiah, the faithful and true Shepherd, to preferve his chofen flock in the hour of danger. He teacheth his afflicted ones to pray; he increafeth their faith—he leadeth them forth befide the waters of comfort. " I " am come," faith he, " that they might " have life, and that they might have it " more abundantly."

Take from us, O bleffed Lord, all unbelief, hardnefs of heart, and contempt of thy word—Open thou our eyes that we may fee the wonders of thy facred truth! Thou, who haft called us with an holy calling—thou, from whofe love, if we have faith, nothing fhall be able to to feparate us—thou, who haft declared, that to them who believe in thee there fhall be a performance of all thine exceeding great and precious promifes—teach us, we humbly befeech thee, to walk in thy light, that we may become the children of light: that fo, adorning the doctrine of God our Saviour in all things, we may demonftrate the excellence of our faith by the purity of our virtue; may hold faft our chriftian profeffion without wavering; and, being ftedfaft in faith, and joyful through hope, may at length, by thy mercy, obtain the END OF OUR FAITH, even the falvation of our fouls, through Jefus Chrift our Lord. Amen.

SERMON

SERMON XII.

THE OBJECT OF CHRISTIAN FAITH.

ADVERTISEMENT.

IT is possible that some of the positions contained in the following discourse may be controverted, not only by the enemies of the christian faith, but by some of its friends and professors, who, with the utmost purity of intention, may think differently from the author on the subjects proposed in it for discussion. He has only to say, that all he has written on the occasion, is written under the solemn conviction of his mind, that what he asserts is true. If he should be attacked on the subject, he thinks himself happy, that he is enabled to retire for protection to the adamantine shield of Bishop HORSLEY.

    See his Lordship's admirable Charge, delivered to the Clergy of the Diocese of Rochester, A. D. 1796, p. 18, 19, &c.

SERMON XII.

THE OBJECT OF CHRISTIAN FAITH.

JOHN xiv. 1.

Ye believe in GOD ; *believe also in me.*

THAT all scripture is given by inspiration of God—that, while it is an unerring rule of life, it doth at the same time exhibit a perfect form of sound doctrine, a congregation of assembled *Christians* will not fail joyfully to acknowlege. To the records of truth therefore we must ever have recourse for in-

information, when we would form a right notion of heavenly things. Let us then fearch the fcriptures with unremitting diligence; for in them we know affuredly that we have eternal life, and thefe are they which teftify of the Almighty.

In the words which I have felected for your meditation this day; our Lord addreffes his difciples immediately before his paffion, and encourages them to fupport themfelves through all the afflicting fcenes which were to follow, in hope of future joy, which no man fhould take from them—directing them, as the ground-work of this hope, and this joy, to know the only true God, and Jefus Chrift, the Word made flefh, who was fent from above, and dwelt among men. " Ye believe in God," faith he, "believe " alfo in me."

Under the fanction of this high authority, I fhall endeavour to fhew, that

to

The Object of Christian Faith.

to believe in God, without believing in Christ, is vain and fruitless—nay, that it is impossible—nor shall I scruple the affertion, harsh as it may sound, that he who is not a Christian, is virtually, though not nominally, an Atheist—and that to believe in God and in Christ is one inseparable act of faith; is indeed only one operation of the mind—which, if we allow not that Christ is GOD, can never take place; and therefore the acknowlegement of OUR BLESSED SAVIOUR'S DIVINITY, in which alone our hope of everlasting joy is founded, will be the glorious result of our enquiries. "This," faith our Lord himself, "is life eternal, that they may know thee, the only true God, and Jesus Christ whom thou hast sent."

In discoursing on this subject, I cannot be supposed to extend my arguments to the Pagan, the Jew, or the Mahometan. These, it must be confessed, acknowlege not the true God—but their errors are from the circumſtances of their birth, the prejudices of their education, and the ſituation in which they are placed, rather than from any wilful blindneſs, and ignorance where the means of knowlege are in their power. It is the ſelf-taught, ſelf-ſufficient infidel, who dignifies his wild ſpeculations by the name of Philoſophy, and whoſe ſyſtem excludes from it all the bleſſings of Redemption, whom I would argue guilty of downright atheiſm, in denying the faith of Chriſt.

To underſtand this, let us enquire, What is an Act of Faith?

It is the aſſent of the mind to the certainty of that, which reaſon of itſelf cannot comprehend, nor argument demonſtrate, upon the reliance we have on the authority which declares it to be true. This reliance is "Faith" in its abſtract

stract and general sense—and by means of it, we receive, and avail ourselves of all the promises of everlasting happiness; being firmly convinced of the absolute certainty of that covenant which God hath made with us in Christ Jesus.

Now, to the belief in God, this act of faith is equally necessary, as to the belief in Christ Jesus—Reason, that is, unassisted reason, cannot comprehend, nor, without the help of revelation, can argument demonstrate either the one or the other. But God in his mercy having been pleased to manifest himself to mankind as a Creator, Redeemer, and Sanctifier, we are made capable of receiving the glad tidings of divine truth—we see with the eye of faith bright and glorious objects, which to the eye of sense were invisible—we behold the Charter of our salvation thus written in the most legible characters. God hath given to us eternal life, and this life is in his Son.

I have

SERM.
XII.
I have said, that reason cannot comprehend, nor argument demonstrate, without the help of Revelation, the existence of a God *. The contrary opinion hath been too generally adopted for the good of mankind; but, I think, without sufficient authority. For though there be that are called gods, both in heaven and earth, as there be gods many and lords many, yet it has never been proved that the truth, from which these are only so many deviations, was discovered by unassisted nature. And one unanswerable argument against the possibility of these natural perceptions is, that there are nations now existing, who have not any knowlege of God †—who are to-

* The being and attributes of God are not to be proved or demonstrated from merely natu.al principles without *data*, or by the unassisted powers of human reason. "I BELIEVE IN GOD" is an article of FAITH, as well as "the resurrection of the body.'
Dr. HODGES's Elihu, p. 218.
† The Aborigines of the island of Sumatra, amongst others. See Marsden's History of Sumatra. See also (*inter al.*) Father Gobien's Account of the aboriginal inhabitants of the Ladrone islands.

tally

tally ignorant, that there is a superior Power which governs the universe, and who have not the least idea of religious worship. Now if without revelation *any man* could form a notion of God, *every man* must do so, and the case above stated could not exist. A truth of this nature, if it could be seen by any, would be seen by all; and those gracious manifestations of himself, which God in pity to our infirmities hath from time to time vouchsafed us, would have been unnecessary and superfluous.

But they are not superfluous. "The spirit of man is the candle of the Lord." Until the candle be lighted, where is its usefulness? And this light it cannot be said to have in itself, being indebted for it to the fire, without which it is altogether unprofitable. Thus, with respect to spiritual knowlege, the soul, which by divine assistance can apprehend so much, without ILLUMINATION is able to comprehend nothing. Let the mind of man be enlightened by the power of God, and he is then, and not before, enabled to discern the Creator in His wondrous works. Then doth light arise in the darkness; he no longer gropes in solitude through the midnight gloom, but he steadily pursues the path pointed out to him by his heavenly guide, and he waits patiently till the day dawn, and the shadows fly away—till the Sun of Righteousness arise with healing in his wings.

Whence then did the idols of heathenism derive their origin, if nature could not of itself discover the existence of a God? We must trace their origin to the faint gleam of imperfect tradition, and to the folly, extravagance, and wicked apostasy of those who knew the right way, yet wilfully deviated from it: thus professing themselves to be wise, they became fools—they turned the truth of

The Object of Christian Faith.

SERM. XII.

of God into a lie, and worshipped the creature more than the Creator. In some countries all religious records are absolutely erased—in others, the most monstrous absurdities have taken the place of truth. But most certain it is, that the descendants of *Noah* could not be originally ignorant of that revelation which was given by the Almighty himself to their common ancestor. The more we scrutinize and investigate the superstitions of Paganism, and the rites of idolatrous devotion, the more clearly are we enabled to discover the analogy between those modes of perverted worship, and the ordinances revealed by God; particularly in the leading circumstance of *sacrifice*—which necessarily implies vicarious suffering, and the atonement made by innocence for the expiation of guilt.

In a Christian country, where the worship of God is professed and established,

lished, it is impossible for a man to say, that he has any natural knowlege of a Supreme Being. As well might he assert that he brought with him the gift of language into the world; a proposition which experimental proof has conclusively determined in the negative. From his earliest infancy he must unavoidably have heard the leading doctrines of the truth; and I humbly apprehend, that the error arises from his mistaking these early-received notions for innate ones; there having never been a time within his memory, when his soul was without the idea of God, he contends that it was coeval with his existence, and is inseparable from the nature of man.

In the first instance, where a sincere regard and reverence for the revealed word accompanies the belief of what is called "natural religion;" the doctrine, though erroneous, may perhaps be innocent—

nocent—but, after its well-meaning advocates have defined its limits and extent, the infidel carries it further, and from the same premises deduces most dangerous conclusions. For when, being spoiled by philosophy and self-deceit, after the rudiments of this world, and not after Christ, he begins to walk in a new path, he effects his purpose by withdrawing his assent from those sublime parts of our religion, which require the exercise of faith, properly so called: such as, the doctrine of Redemption—of reconciliation with offended Heaven—of GOD incarnate, visiting in great humility a world of sinners, to accomplish the work of their salvation—of the means he made use of in their behalf—his life, his sufferings, his death, his resurrection, his return to his Almighty Father.

Having thus alienated himself from the *faith*, he abandons likewise the *hope* of a Christian. Then denies he that
blessed

SERM. XII.

blessed and comfortable doctrine of "the forgiveness of sins," through the blood of a Mediator—" the resurrection of the body," whereof Christ's resurrection was a sign and an assurance—and " the life everlasting," which shall be the inheritance of all true believers in the kingdom of the Great God and our Saviour Jesus Christ.

Meanwhile he tells us on all occasions, that he considers himself as believing in God, the Father and Creator of the world, after whose name he calls himself, and whose religion he professes under the name of *pure deism*—a religion without a service, without a temple, without a sacrifice, without a Redeemer, without a Comforter, without prayer, without praise, without faith, without hope, without sanctification, without salvation—without every thing!

But

But it is surely far too great a concession to allow, that he is a believer in GOD. For the God whom he affects to adore must be either the true God, or a false one; and if a false one, then is he not God, but a phantom impiously set up in opposition to the everlasting Jehovah. Now gospel-truth, or the religion of the Bible, declares, " that the Son of " God is come, and hath given us un- " derstanding, that we may know him " that is true; and we are in him that " is true, even in his son Jesus Christ— " THIS IS THE TRUE GOD, and everlasting " Life. Little children, keep yourselves " from idols!"

If this is the true God, it follows, that all other gods are false; and he who denies the truths of Christianity, must pardon us for pronouncing him to be absolutely without God, inasmuch as he is without the only true object of religious adoration.

R   Thus;

Thus, in a state of dark uncertainty, with no sure ground on which he may walk, no fixed principles whereby he may direct himself, wanders the deluded infidel—in a wilderness, where there is no way; in a stormy sea, without a compass; in an unknown country, without a guide. And why? Because instead of making his reason subject to God, he would make God subject to his reason; because he most unthankfully uses the greatest of all possible gifts in opposition to the merciful and benignant Giver.

Let us now betake ourselves to more pleasing contemplations—let us consider that blessedness which the religion of a crucified Saviour brings with it, and that comfort which revelation imparts, when it teaches us, that to believe in God and in Christ Jesus is " one faith," eternally and inseparably the same.

In the beginning, when the firſt framed father of all men became a living ſoul, the Almighty deigned to hold perſonal converſe with him, and to teach thoſe important truths, which his reaſon, unaſſiſted by ſuch divine communication, could never have been able to diſcover. No ſooner did man at the fall become a ſinner, than God in his mercy became a Saviour—and the promiſe of redemption through Chriſt Jeſus was made to Adam and to his progeny by immediate *revelation* from heaven.

That the generations which were to come, and the children who were then unborn, might know theſe things, and that their hearts might be impreſſed with a ſenſe of the kindneſs of God, the divine oracles were ſubſequently given, and were carefully preſerved. The inſpired penmen, moved by the Holy Ghoſt, from age to age recorded the marvellous acts of the Almighty, and de-

delivered to mankind the doctrines of truth and of life. Patriarchs and Prophets died in faith, not having received the promises, but having seen them afar off, and being persuaded of their certainty, through the word of God which standeth sure for ever. Thus Abraham rejoiced to see the day of Christ, and he saw it, and was glad. Thus we hear Job, proclaiming with the voice of rapture, "I know that my REDEEMER liveth!" and David, who knew the knowlege of the most High, declaring, with a reference to the Messiah, that " Truth should spring " out of the earth, and Righteousness " should look down from heaven."

At length the promised and expected Saviour appeared—literally fulfilling all prophecies, and bringing with him the substance of those good things which were only foreshadowed by the law and its ordinances. Every cloud of obscurity was now removed—our Lord manifested

The Object of Christian Faith.

fested himself openly to the world, and explained to all mankind the things concerning himself: " I and my Father are " one." " He that hath seen me, hath " seen the Father." " Ye believe in God, " believe also in me *."

Let us compare spiritual things with spiritual, and, by way of comment on these divine words, have recourse to the language of St. Paul when addressing his Corinthian converts, on the atonement made by Christ for the sins of his people.

" All things," faith he, " are of God,
" who hath reconciled us to himself by
" Jesus Christ, and hath given to us the
" ministry of reconciliation, to wit,
" THAT GOD WAS IN CHRIST, reconciling
" the world unto himself, not imputing
" their trespasses unto them:" " For he
" hath

* See Sermon III. p. 66.

SERM. XII.

" hath made Him to be sin for us, who knew no sin, that we might be made the righteousness of God IN HIM."

The above is the sum and substance of Christianity—the immoveable Rock, to which our faith and hope should for ever adhere.

If then, in point of fact, man has no natural knowlege of God—if the varieties of worship throughout the world have their derivation from the original Fountain of Truth, and are only so many perversions from that right way wherein all were instructed to walk—if God revealed himself to our first parent in his Paradise, that he might obey and live; and again, after his defection, that he might believe and be saved—if the covenant of mercy, the reconciliation of an offended God to his creatures, has for its only basis the all-powerful efficacy of a Redeemer's merits; then they who reject

that

that Redeemer, do reject the true God revealed to them from heaven—and not worshipping the true God, they in fact worship no God at all; the object of their idolatrous reverence being exactly on a level with the Moloch and Chemosh of those Gentile nations, who are declared by the Apostle to have paid their adorations to devils, and not to God.

And is the union of the Father and the Son, in the Divine Nature, together with the Holy Spirit, mysterious, and above human comprehension? Let us only reflect a moment on the high and mysterious nature of the subject. How can man, who is a worm, be able to conceive a just notion of the omnipotent God? Or, if we should for a moment suppose such knowlege attainable, where would there be room for that faith, without which it is impossible to please God, if the things of heaven, which no man can

can search out, were in their nature capable of mathematical demonstration?

Much yet remains unsaid, on this important and interesting topic; but (left we should be accused of dwelling with undue prolixity on subjects too intricate for human investigation) after impressing on your minds the necessary truth, that to consider Christ as God is not a matter of abstract theory, but of positive duty, let us bring the application of this doctrine home to our hearts. Let us admonish you, that the followers of the holy Jesus are, by virtue of their profession, engaged to the practice of every virtue—particularly those eminent *christian* Virtues, Humility, Mercy, Meekness, Patience, Charity: that they who are strong in the faith, that lively and invigorating faith which demonstrates itself by holiness of life, must be careful to maintain good works, and to bring forth the fruits of righteousness.

If we neglect thefe, our faith is made void, and the promife, as far as concerns our falvation, will be of none effect. But if we work the works of him who hath fent us, in the full conviction of our fouls, that our imperfect fervices will be accepted through the merits of that ever-bleffed Saviour on whom we have believed, then fhall we perfevere with joy in the path of duty, and at the laft we fhall not be difappointed of our hope.

When we are oppreffed by tribulation and reproach, we fhall look for deliverance to Him whofe forrow was beyond the capacity of our fuffering; and fhall be affured, that if we endure unto the end, our forrows, like thofe of our gracious mafter, will be turned into joy. When we are called on to fuftain the laft dreadful conflict, ftill is He the ftrength of our hearts, and our portion for ever. Our flefh fhall reft in hope. We fhall be
planted

SERM. XII. planted in the likeness of his resurrection.

In a word, are we poor? are we dejected? are we friendless? are we despised, oppressed, and persecuted? are we suffering under infirmities of body or of mind? are we visited by pining sickness? or do we bewail the loss of those who were dearer to us than ourselves? in all these, and in all other cases of affliction, whatsoever plague, whatsoever misery, whatsoever danger there may be, still the comfortable voice of the Redeemer of mankind chears us through this vale of sorrows,

Let not your hearts be troubled—YE BELIEVE IN GOD—BELIEVE ALSO IN ME!

SERMON

SERMON XIII.

THE TRIUMPHS OF CHRISTIAN FAITH.

SERMON

SERMON XIII.

THE TRIUMPHS OF CHRISTIAN FAITH.

---

1 JOHN v.—5.

Who is he that overcometh the world, but he that believeth that Jesus is the Son of God?

"No man, Lord! without that faith
"which centers folely in thee, there is
"none that hath the victory—none that
"overcometh—none that doeth good,
"no, not one. Whenfoever we call upon
"thee, then fhall our adverfaries be put
"to flight—this we know, for God is on
"our fide."

The

SERM.
XIII.

The world is an enemy, formidable indeed, but not invincible—an enemy, with whom we muſt of neceſſity contend, but over whom, with the divine aſſiſtance, we may be triumphant and victorious—an enemy, whoſe purpoſes are defeated by Chriſtian fortitude—an enemy, whoſe power is annihilated by Chriſtian Faith.

The members of Chriſt's holy church militant here on earth, cannot but be well acquainted with the malignity of that rancorous foe with whom they have to combat. It is the prince, or, as he is elſewhere called, the god of this evil world, who ſets himſelf in array againſt them. Cloſe by the ſide of this formidable antagoniſt we behold his auxiliary powers—the luſt of the fleſh, the luſt of the eye, and the pride of life. The glaring pomps by which mortals are dazzled in the ſun-ſhine of proſperity, and are allured to their deſtruction, glitter in his hand; the lying vanities,

vanities, which set themselves in direct opposition to christian humility, are waving, in impious defiance, over his head. ' Against this opponent, whose assaults are carried on with more inveterate malice because he knoweth that he hath but a short time—against the WORLD, with all its unlawful gratifications, all its corrupt propensities, and all its unhallowed pursuits, we are to wage incessant and perpetual warfare; and it is only on condition of being victorious in the conflict, that we can form any hope of being partakers of that exceeding and eternal weight of glory, reserved for the redeemed of God.

' The religion of Jesus Christ therefore, and the maxims of this sinful world, being in direct and pointed opposition to each other, no compromise can be made between them. We cannot bow the knee to this gilded idol, and at the same time preserve the favour of the God of heaven.

We

SERM. XIII.

We cannot with impunity offer divided homage. We cannot halt between two opinions. The oracles of divine truth found in our ears; they speak to us, in language not to be misunderstood, whether we will hear, or whether we will forbear: "Love not the world, neither "the things that are in the world." The precept is clear and unequivocal: no ingenuity can evade it; no sophistry can explain it away. "If any man love the "world, the love of the Father is not in "him."

We must therefore be fully convinced, if our souls are not hardened against conviction, that the contest to which we are called by the profession of our faith is a contest of the utmost importance—and I must again impress it on your minds, that it is a contest, to which there can be no dubious, no uncertain issue. If we do not overcome the world, the world will infallibly overcome us—there is no room for temporizing conceſſions—there is no poſſibility of entering into treaty with our antagoniſt. " What agreement hath the temple of God with idols? What concord hath Chriſt with Belial?" What have we to do with peace, ſeeing the deluſions of this perfidious world, and its witchcrafts are ſo many?

If we are endued with true Chriſtian courage we ſhall not deſpair—we ſhall not abandon "the ſuccours which reaſon offereth *," becauſe we have in view the full extent of our danger. On the contrary, all our hopes increaſe, and all our beſt energies riſe, in proportion to the difficulties we have to encounter. Let it not then in the preſent inſtance check the ardour of our exertions—let it rather add ſtrength and vigour to our arm, that we find ourſelves engaged in a conflict, from which we cannot, without incurring certain deſtruction, retreat

* Wiſd. xvii. 12.

or recede. My christian brethren, there is no alternative here—no medium between ignominy and triumph. Death and life are set before us; the one for the punishment of our defeat, the other for the reward of our victory.

Such are the terms on which we engage in this our spiritual warfare—where we wrestle, not only against flesh and blood, but against principalities, against powers, against the rulers of the darkness of this world—against every high thing that exalteth itself in opposition to God—against every thought, which is not in subjection to the law of Christ. In this contest, if we do not prevail, we are undone—if our faith fails, we are scared at the boisterous tempest—we sink in the mighty waters, and the stream goeth over our soul. Woe therefore to them that are of faint hearts and of weak hands, who turn aside with the deluded multitude from the path of glory, and will not follow the Captain of their Salvation in that illustrious course, which leads to permanent and unfading joy!

" He that faith he abideth in Christ " ought himself also so to walk, even as " HE walked.". By this we know, that we must tread in the footsteps of our blessed Saviour, if we would partake with him of his heavenly kingdom; and that on our imitation (as far as mortal frailty admits) of His perfect example we must depend for our improvement in grace, and our elevation to heights of virtue no otherwise attainable *.

Meanwhile, in all our troubles, in all our sufferings here upon earth, the purest balm of comfort, the most precious

---

* See p. 339 of Wilberforce's " Practical View of " Christianity:" concerning which the author of these discourses would attempt to leave his opinion on record, were he not aware that it is a work which rises infinitely superior to all human praise:

" Qualis sit, ILLE DIES indicabit."

fountain of hope, ariſes from our remembrance, that Jeſus, the Son of God, was, in his own perſon, as the ſon of man, called to ſuſtain a ſimilar conflict, and was crowned with the moſt deciſive victory: "For he himſelf went not up to joy, but firſt he ſuffered pain; he entered not into his glory before he was crucified. So truly our way to eternal joy is to ſuffer here with Chriſt, and our door to enter into eternal life is gladly to die with Chriſt; that we may riſe again from death, and dwell with him in everlaſting life*." " Theſe things have I ſpoken unto you"—it is his own gracious word—" theſe things " have I ſpoken unto you, that in me " ye might have peace. In the world ye " ſhall have tribulation; but be of good " cheer! I HAVE OVERCOME THE WORLD." From the habitation of his holineſs and of his glory, our Saviour calls to us— bids us perſevere with undaunted reſo-

* Office for the Viſitation of the Sick.

lution—

lution—tells us what will be the bright meed of the conqueror. "To him that "overcometh will I give to eat of the "tree of life which is in the midſt of the "Paradiſe of God. He that overcometh "ſhall not be hurt by the ſecond death. "To him will I give to eat of the hidden "manna—and I will give unto him the "morning ſtar. Him that overcometh "will I make as a pillar in the temple "of God. I will confeſs his name before "my Father, and before his angels. To "him that overcometh will I grant to "ſit with me in my throne, even as I "alſo overcame, and am ſet down with "my Father in his throne *."

Shall we then, my beloved in Chriſt, ſhall we ſhrink ingloriouſly from a warfare, in which we are animated by ſuch great and precious promiſes as theſe? Do not our hearts burn within us, while we thus hear recited the joy that is ſet

* See Rev. chap. ii—iii.

before

SERM. XIII. before us—while we have the unutterable blifs of being affured, that Chrift is in us the hope of glory? Though our enemies are numerous and mighty—though they approach us in divers ways, and carry on their attacks in every poffible direction—though at one time they openly affault, and at another time infidiously betray, yet let not our hearts be troubled, neither let them be afraid. We are clad in celeftial armour, and are able to refift them. We will triumph in the name of the Lord our God. He will give a banner to fuch as fear him, that they may be victorious *becaufe of the truth*. The Lord is our refuge, and our God is the ftrength of our confidence. This is the victory that overcometh the world, even our FAITH.

Would you enquire, of what *nature* is the faith, which leads to meet an exceeding and eternal weight of glory? Would you afk, who is it that thus
goeth

goeth forth, conquering and to conquer? The words of my text prefent you with a conclufive anfwer. He is thus victorious—he thus triumphs—*who believes that Jefus is the Son of God.* It is the faith of the CHRISTIAN which fupports him in all dangers, and carries him through all temptations. Among all the viciffitudes of life this faith conducts him in fafety; and when he walks through the valley of the fhadow of death it preferves him from the fear of evil. The glorious company of the apoftles—the goodly fellowfhip of the prophets—the noble army of martyrs—the faints of God from the commencement of time to the prefent hour, have taken this invincible fhield, and have ever been fafe under its protection. Knowing on whom they believed, and being perfuaded, that he was both able and willing to fave them to the uttermoft; they chofe the good part, which no malice, no violence, could take away from them. The world was

was thus crucified unto them, and they unto the world. During the continuance of their warfare they committed the keeping of their fouls unto their God ; at its termination, they refigned their fpirits with confidence into the nands of the fame faithful Creator, and moft merciful Redeemer.

While we meditate on thefe things—while we give ourfelves wholly unto them, mortality feems to be fwallowed up in life. Where, at fuch a moment, are earthly joys, and earthly forrows ? They are excluded. By what law ? of works ? Nay, but by the law of faith. Borne on her celeftial wings, we are elevated to a region fo pure, fo unclouded, fo ethereal, that the low and vapourifh mifts of this prefent world cannot approach to annoy us. We are removed for a time out of the reach of the ftorms and tempefts of life—" eternal funfhine" is beaming on our heads—we anticipate

anticipate the blessed hour, when He who hath overcome the sharpness of death shall open the kingdom of heaven to all believers. Beholding, with open face, the glory of the Lord, we are changed into the same image, from glory to glory, even as by the Spirit of the Lord.

But, from contemplations like these, however sublime, however animating, we must descend to the scene of our existing trials. We may indeed cry out, as did the enraptured apostle (when he saw the bright vision on mount Tabor) " Lord, it is good for us to be here!" But we are to be reminded, that the crown is preceded by a conflict—that labour is preparatory to our rest—that we must work the work of Him that hath sent us while it is day; a work of no trivial concern; a work which may not be laid aside and resumed at pleasure—that our time of probation, of difficulty,

SERM.
XIII.
ficulty, of warfare, is not over—that we have duties of the higheſt magnitude to fulfil ; a character of infinite importance to ſuſtain—that, before we are called to a participation of everlaſting happineſs, we muſt live the life, and we muſt die the death, of the righteous.

Here then we perceive, in all its bleſſedneſs, the ineſtimable value of our high calling of God in Chriſt Jeſus. When the world beſets us, accompanied by its cares and anxieties, its wiles and temptations, its idle day-dreams of hope, its deluſive phantoms of terror, when we are threatened with an impending weight whoſe fall, coming ſuddenly and at an inſtant, would cruſh us to atoms, FAITH and HOPE ſhelter us under their wings. They avert the meditated evil, and turn it into certain and infallible good. They direct our thoughts to future and eternal joy. They call on us to behold the glory of God, and Jeſus, ſtanding at the right hand

hand of God. They point out to us the way in which we are to walk, and the work which it is our duty to perform. They enable us to poſſeſs our ſouls in patience. They ſuſtain our drooping and wearied ſpirits. They wipe away all tears from our eyes—or elſe they teach thoſe tears to flow with emotions ſo chaſtened, with reſignation ſo meek, that ſorrow itſelf loſes all its bitterneſs, and while we ſtill preſerve the tendereſt ſenſibilities of our nature, we conſecrate them, with duteous ſubmiſſion, on the altar of Chriſt.

Theſe are the glorious fruits of our holy religion—theſe are the bleſſings vouchſafed to the believer in the hour of his adverſity. In compariſon with gifts thus precious, with benefits thus unfading, what has airy and fantaſtic pleaſure, what has ſtern and gloomy infidelity to beſtow? Take away our chriſtian *faith*, and we are like waves of the ſea, driven by the wind, and toſſed. Take away our chriſtian *hope*, and

SERM.
XIII.
and in very deed we are of all men moſt miſerable. In the multitude of the ſorrows which we have in our hearts, thy comforts alone, O bleſſed Jeſus, can refreſh and ſuſtain the ſoul. Tell the poor ſufferer, that his gracious Saviour has gone in the thorny way before him— that his temporary afflictions are a prelude to eternal joy—that his warfare will ſoon be accompliſhed—that his iniquities, through the mercy of God in Chriſt, will be freely pardoned—and you revive his fainting heart. Light ariſes to him in the darkneſs. He lifts up his head with joy, knowing, that his redemption draweth nigh. Can the ſenſualiſt, or the unbeliever, ſuggeſt to him motives of conſolation adequate to theſe, when he is in ſickneſs, in poverty, in ſorrow ? when his proſpects of happineſs are diſappointed ? when his beſt earthly bleſſings are vaniſhed out of his ſight ? Under theſe afflicting viſitations, will the wounded ſoul be capable of obtaining

ing relief from cold and metaphyfical theories, or moral effays on the eternal fitnefs of things? Should not a people feek unto their God? Is there any name under heaven given unto man, in whom or through whom, we can receive help, or joy, or comfort, or falvation, fave only the name of our Lord Jefus Chrift? Bleffed Saviour, what is our hope? Truly our hope is even, truly our hope is only, in thee.

To this hope, as an anchor of the foul, let us adhere; and we fhall ftand faft for ever and ever. Let it be our conftant affociate through our lives; and from it, even in death, we fhall not be divided. Then—then to overcome the world, is the laft, the beft, the greateft privilege of them who believe that Jefus is the Son of God. With a view to this awful confummation they direct all their conduct—with a reference to it, every thought, every word, every action, is regulated.

regulated. Sweet is the tranquillity of that heart, which can rely on the love of Chrift in its clofing hours, and which fhrinks not from approaching diffolution. To have furmounted this terrour—to have made an holy life thus preparatory to an happy death, is a ftate of perfection, in which man is indeed little lower than an angel. How fublime and interefting is the fpectacle—how exquifite are the emotions which are felt by thofe who witnefs it, when the Chriftian, full of years, and full of honour, having glorified the name of God on earth, and having finifhed the work given him to perform, awaits, in holy patience, the fummons of his Redeemer! In the clofe of his life, as well as in its progrefs, he inftructs, he comforts, he edifies thofe around him. His old age is like the mild radiance of an autumnal evening—calm, bright, ferene—clear, even to the laft moments of the fetting fun. Death is to fuch an one the entrance into life, and

the

the grave is the gate of Heaven. He expires, but he expires in the arms of victory: now is come salvation, and strength, and the kingdom of the Lord, and the power of Christ. The weapons of his warfare are exchanged for the bright robe of peace—a crown of life is set upon his head, and sorrow is turned into everlasting joy.

THANKS BE TO GOD, WHO THUS GIVETH THE VICTORY, THROUGH OUR LORD JESUS CHRIST.

Therefore, my beloved brethren, be ye stedfast, unmoveable, always abounding in the work of the Lord, forasmuch as ye know that your labour is not in vain in the Lord.

SERMON

SERMON XIV.

THE FOUNDATION OF CHRISTIAN HOPE.

SERMON XIV.

THE FOUNDATION OF CHRISTIAN HOPE.

HEBREWS xiii. 5.

"*I will never leave thee, nor forsake thee.*"

THUS speaketh to his poor weak afflicted creatures, the GOD of Truth, the GOD of Peace, the GOD of Hope, the GOD of Comfort. He hath said, and his word is true—he hath promised and there shall be a performance of his promise—I WILL NEVER LEAVE THEE, NOR FORSAKE THEE. This God is our God for ever and ever: he will be our Guide, even unto death.

SERM. XIV.

Why then art thou caſt down, O my ſoul, and why art thou difquieted within me ? Why wilt thou not put thy truſt in God, and give him thanks, who is the health of thy countenance, and thy GOD ?

Confidered in himſelf, man is the moſt pitiable object in the world. He is weak and feeble in his nature, yet is he expoſed to a variety of ſorrows. He is prone to evil, and befet with temptations, yet is he unable to keep himſelf from falling; or, if he fall, he hath no ſtrength to ariſe. But man, under the protection of God—man, aided by the omnipotent Jehovah, is a new creature. Former things are done away : behold, all things are become new ! His weakneſs is made ſtrong—his feet are upholden that they ſhould not ſtumble—his ſorrow is turned into joy. They who lean upon their God, and rely on His heavenly grace, are evermore defended

by

The Foundation of Christian Hope.

by his mighty power*. The tender plant, which would otherwise be exposed to the tempestuous blast, or lie prostrate on the ground, subject to the step of each passing traveller, adheres to the majestic oak, and finds protection under its branches. By that strength it is supported—under that shadow it is safe. The winds have no power to rend, or the foot to crush it. It flourishes in peace and security, lifts up its head above the reach of danger, and sustains unhurt all the terrors of the storm.

Let us then, my beloved brethren, apply the inestimable blessings of CHRISTIAN HOPE to those cases of affliction which meet us in every path, while we sojourn upon earth—cases, where our own resources fail us, and where mankind are frequently unable, and more frequently unwilling, to afford us assistance. Christian hope imparts to us its succour under all our sorrows. It sup-

* Collect for the 5th Sunday after Epiphany.

ports us under misfortunes and calamities. It comforts us, when we are mourning under the moſt ſevere viſitations. It ſtrengthens and ſuſtains us amidſt the perſecutions of our enemies. It pours the balm of comfort into our minds, when they are torn by treachery and ingratitude. Like a miniſtering angel, it ſoothes us in the hour of ſickneſs. From the bed of death it ſends us on our way rejoicing. In all things it makes us more than conquerors through Him who hath loved us.

I. We form hopes of worldly happineſs—innocent hopes, but precarious in themſelves, for we know not even how to wiſh aright; and precarious in their accompliſhment, as being ſubject to perpetual diſappointments. It ſometimes pleaſes God to bleſs us in our purſuits, and to make all our goings proſperous. At other times it is his heavenly will to ſtrike at the root of our fondeſt wiſhes, and

and to lay all our vain projects in the duft. If the Almighty, for the trial of our faith, fhould exercife us with troubles, are we therefore to repine and murmur? Are we to complain of our God, becaufe his knowlege fruftrates the purpofes of our ignorance? Though our hopes prove frail and vifionary—though the objects of our expectation be as the morning cloud, and as the early dew that paffeth away, yet may we rejoice in the Lord, we may glory in the God of our falvation. The abundant riches of his grace may be our portion: what more then can we require? We have free accefs to the treafures of divine mercy: how then can we lack any thing? It is the Lord, who hath called us to our prefent fufferings. It is the Lord, who can fupport us under them. It is the Lord, to whom we muft look for our deliverance. It is the Lord—let him do what feemeth him good! "Be ftrong," he cries, "and fear not—*I will never leave thee* forsake thee. In a little wrath I hid my face from thee for a moment, but with everlasting kindness will I have mercy on thee, faith the Lord thy Redeemer. Fear not, for thou shalt not be ashamed : for my loving kindness shall not depart from thee; neither shall the covenant of thy peace be removed, faith the Lord who hath mercy on thee."

II. Again. The sacred ties of nature must, in the course of time, be dissolved. Those connections from which we derive our purest earthly blessings must have a period. Our happiness, and the objects in whom it is centered, will pass away, and be no more seen. The thought is awful; it is replete with solicitude: such is nevertheless the unalterable condition of our mortal nature. Either we lament the death of a friend or brother—or we go heavily, mourning for the protectors of our infancy, the guides and guardians of our youth—or
" the

"the defire of our eyes is taken away at a ftroke"—or we fhed bitter tears over the remains of thofe to whom we had ourfelves looked for the laft folemn offices of pious duty. If any of thefe fevere and dreadful inflictions from Heaven are upon us—if our home, once the feat of joy and gladnefs, is forlorn and defolate, with no interruption to the gloomy filence, but our own expreffions of agonizing forrow, are we therefore left alone? No—we are not alone, becaufe the Almighty is with us. He is the fountain of life and immortality—he is the treafure of blifs inexhauftible and everlafting. He, in himfelf, in all his attributes, in all his difpenfations towards us, is unchangeable. The comfort which we derive from his bleffed prefence cannot be taken away by any event, cannot be difturbed by any calamity. Nay, he is more peculiarly at hand to help us, when our hearts are bowed down with anguifh. He doth not willingly

SERM.
XIV.
lingly grieve nor afflict the children of men. *When my father and my mother forsake me* (faith David) that is, when they leave this tranfitory world, and can no longer blefs me with their parental care, *then the Lord taketh me up.* God is in a peculiar manner prefent, when trouble is hard at hand, and there is none to help us. He is a Father to the fatherlefs—he defendeth the caufe of the widow. His eyes are open to behold their grief—his ears attend to the prayers which they pour forth to him in the bitternefs of their forrows. He will love them with an everlafting love; and if they truft in him they fhall not be deftitute. Relying on God, and looking forward to that which is perfect, they fuftain the trials of this prefent ftate of imperfection with becoming fortitude. They hear the bleffed voice of comfort piercing the clouds, and defcending as it were from heaven, *I will never leave thee nor forfake thee.* Thus fuccoured, thus

thus encouraged, they wait patiently for that day, which shall restore to them the blessings of which they are only for a time deprived: and they anticipate those blessings with more perfect pleasure, because, when again restored, they will be taken away no more. Sorrow and mourning shall then flee away; joy and gladness shall endure for ever and ever.

III. Are our enemies daily in hand to swallow us up? Are they who hate us wrongfully many in number? Let us put on the armour of righteousness—let us go forth in the strength of the Lord God. If the Lord be for us, who shall prevail against us? God will turn his hand against our adversaries; he will put them to confusion that hate us. During a time, however, he may see fit to leave us in their power—it may be his pleasure that our enemies should be prosperous and mighty. For let not any man imagine, that he can so direct the tenour of his life, as to escape the envenomed shafts of detraction, the open attacks of malice, the secret snares of treachery. Yet He who was manifested to destroy the works of the devil—he who came down from heaven to teach us the way thither—he who suffered such contradictions of sinners against himself—he, even our Saviour, made it the first object of his mission to preach the gospel of PEACE. " Love your enemies—bless them that curse you—do good to them that hate you—and pray for them which despitefully use you and persecute you—that ye may be the children of your Father which is in heaven!"

From whence then come wars and contentions? From the prevalence of sin—from the despite done to the Spirit of grace—from the suggestions of the powers of darkness. It cannot be denied, and it must not be dissembled, that all who would live godly in Christ Jesus, while

while they continue in this prefent world, muft fuffer perfecution. Nor is it only as followers of our bleffed Lord that we are objects of the malice and defpitefulnefs of evil men. Even in matters unconnected with religion, the tongue of flander mifreprefents our conduct—the eye of jealoufy looks with malignity at our fuccefs—caufelefs cenfures are heaped upon us—refentments are returned for our good-will: unjuft infinuations, ungrounded fufpicions, eftrangement of affection, all in their turns militate againft our peace: If we are overcome by their attacks, if we fall from our own ftedfaftnefs, then the foe to human happinefs rejoiceth—then the adverfaries of Jehovah take occafion to blafpheme. But God forbid, that becaufe iniquity abounds, our love, or our patience fhould wax cold! God forbid, that becaufe of earthly enemies we fhould forget our heavenly Friend! In fix afflictions He will deliver us; in feven, they

they shall not approach to hurt us. He will redeem the souls of his servants. Though the wicked speak evil of them, whisper against them, and even consult together to take away their life, still he commands them to put their trust in Him with unshaken confidence. "Be not afraid," saith he, " of them who kill the body, and after that have no more that they can do! Thine enemies are only suffered to make a trial of thy faith —they can do nothing at all to hurt thee, except it be permitted them from above. Trust thou in the Lord, and stay upon thy God. Be thou faithful unto death, and I will give thee a crown of life."

IV. But what is the envy, hatred, malice, and uncharitableness of our enemies, when compared with the defection and ingratitude of those whom we have loved, of those whom we have entrusted with every thought of our unsuspicious hearts? This surely is a far more bitter ingredient

ent in the cup of human misery. The royal Psalmist mentions it as an affliction almost too great for human nature to sustain. "It was not an open enemy that did me this dishonour; *for then I could have borne it:* neither was it mine adversary that did magnify himself against me; for then peradventure I might have hid myself from him: but it was even thou my companion, my guide, and my own familiar friend!" When we suffer under this complicated woe, we can form some faint idea of what our blessed Saviour endured, when he was betrayed by one Apostle, denied by another, basely deserted by all. Yet this he underwent for our sakes: and can we not then be content to partake of his sufferings? Can we not, by the assistance of divine grace, be calm and patient, be meek and submissive, as he was? We are not called on to sustain the conflict without his aid. The Lord, even the most mighty God, hath spoken, "*I will never leave t* nor forsake thee." Can a man forget his benefactor, his patron, his protector? Yes, they may forget; but thy Protector, thy Patron, thy Benefactor, will not forget thee. If thou faint in the day of adversity, thy strength is small. God is still thy Father, O Christian, though they whom thou hast loved be ignorant of thee—though they whom thou hast benefited acknowlege thee not. God is still thy Father, thy Redeemer, his name is from everlasting.

V. " Blessed is he who trusteth in the Lord, and whose hope the Lord is." We have a conflict to sustain; and it will require all our confidence, all our faith, to enable us to endure it. We must walk through the valley of the shadow of death. If we have made God our friend, if we have remembered our Creator in the days of our youth—have offered thanksgivings unto God in our prosperity—have paid our vows unto the

Most

Most High—then, if we call upon him in the time of trouble, he will hear us, and we shall praise him. But unto the ungodly saith God, " Because I have called, and ye refused—I have stretched out my hands, and ye have not regarded—I also will laugh at your calamity; I will mock when your fear cometh—when your fear cometh as desolation, and your destruction cometh as a whirlwind—when distress and anguish cometh upon you!"

Here then at least it must be owned, that all resources of consolation fail us, but such as are drawn from God. Philosophy cannot calm the expiring spirit. An infidel is a wretched companion, when the soul is about to depart from its earthly mansion, when there is but one step betwixt us and death. Then it is, that our hope in Christ sustains us under all our sorrows—alleviates our pains—bids us forget the troubles of the moment, because they are only a pathway to our glory—tells us, that God is our friend, and the Moſt High God our Redeemer—that we have no danger to apprehend, no evil to fear—that He who hath made and hath fuſtained us hitherto will continue ſtill to ſupport and to deliver us—that *he will never leave us, nor forſake us:* but will make his ſtrength perfect in our weakneſs, even in our laſt agonies—in the hour of death—in the day of judgment. " I have loved thee (faith an illuſtrious ſaint of God) I have ſerved thee, and now I come unto thee, O my Saviour! Thou haſt called unto thee thoſe that labour and are heavy laden: thou haſt promiſed to give them reſt. O bleſſed exchange, when the ſoul will be ſummoned from this vain and fleeting world to the ſociety of kindred ſpirits, of angels, and juſt men made perfect, when glory and immortality will be her attendants, and her habitation the palace of the King of kings! This will be a life worth dying for indeed. Thus to exiſt, though but in proſpect, is joy, gladneſs, tranſport, extaſy! Fired with the view

view of this tranfcendent happinefs, and triumphant in CHRISTIAN HOPE, how is it poffible to forbear crying out, "O Death, why art thou fo long in coming? why tarry the wheels of thy chariot?"

With profpects like thefe, what have we to fear? What, but our own unworthinefs, our own imperfection, frailty, and infirmity—left we fall from our ftedfaftnefs, and ceafe to become fit objects of divine mercy? Againft a danger like this we have need of all our caution, all our moft vigilant exertions. And here we muft implore the affiftance of our God, that he would profper the work of his own hands—that having begun what is good in us, he would perform it unto the day of Jefus Chrift—that He, who hath promifed to be with us even to the end of the world, would keep us from falling, and prefent us faultlefs in the prefence of his glory with exceeding joy—

that, becaufe through the weaknefs of our mortal nature we can do no good thing without his continued prefence, he would " grant us the help of his grace, that in keeping his commandments we may pleafe him both in will and deed, through Jefus Chrift our Lord." Amen.

SERMON XV.

THE PROMISE OF CHRISTIAN HOPE.

SERMON XV.

THE PROMISE OF CHRISTIAN HOPE.

MICAH ii.—10.

"*Arise ye, and depart—for this is not your rest.*"

THESE words spake the Lord by his prophet to the house of Jacob, the children of adoption, that highly favoured people which once he distinguished as his own. But they are words of no limited, no particular application. I wish to consider them as even now addressed to all who have received the glad tidings of salvation, to all on whom the light of the glorious gospel hath shined. They are words equally profitable for instruction, for reproof, for comfort: not merely at the close of our earthly warfare, when, full of anxious solicitude, and trembling on the confines of immortality, we prepare to meet our God; but through the whole duration of our life—through the various and changing scenes of our existence—whatever is our state, whatever our portion in this world—whether we are perplexed by its difficulties, enamoured of its delusions, or sinking under its sorrows, still we hear the heavenly voice speaking unto us, as unto strangers and sojourners upon the earth, " Arise ye, and depart—for this is not your rest."

But this address is capable of another interpretation, still more solemn, still more sublime. It is applicable to that awful

awful hour, when, amidſt the laſt agonies of the univerſe, the jar of elements, and the wreck of created nature, the voice of the Archangel and the trump of God ſhall ſound—the dead ſhall hear, and ſhall live. " Awake, ye that dwell in the duſt. *Ariſe and depart*—theſe manſions are not always to detain you. *This is not your* perpetual *reſt*. Awake from the ſleep of death, and ſtand before the throne of your omnipotent Saviour; for he is come, for he is come to judge the earth—and with righteouſneſs to judge the world, and the people with equity."

Theſe are the momentous ſubjects of ſerious and ſacred meditation, which I would ſubmit to your reflection this day.

The words, as I have already declared to you, are the words of God—the voice is the voice of admonition, of exhortation, of hope. We are called from the tranſient joys, from the ſhadowy ſorrows of

SERM. XV.

of mortality, to the permanent felicity, to the refulgent light of heaven—we are incited to loosen by degrees these chains which now rivet us to our earthly prison, and with our full soul to aspire after the glorious liberty of the children of God.

Whether in point of fact the words of my text are experimentally true, is a question which may be decided even without referring them to the authority of divine inspiration. Tell me, my brethren, and weigh well the force of the enquiry before your hearts make the answer, tell me, whether you are not fully convinced, that your rest is not here? How fondly soever you may be attached to the world—how liberal soever indulgent Providence may have been in showering upon you every earthly blessing, tell me, as ye would answer in the presence of the Almighty, if ye are completely in possession of that repose repofe for which you languish, or whether you are not often ready to exclaim with the Pſalmiſt, " Oh that I had wings like a dove! for then would I flee away and be at reſt?" There can be no doubt whatever as to the reply. The ſoul is framed for immortality, and nothing ſhort of immortality can fully ſatisfy it.

If this truth does not at firſt ſight bring conviction to your minds, conſider ſeriouſly and attentively the inſufficiency of all ſublunary *pleaſures.*

But firſt, with diſcriminating juſtice, eraſe from the account every ſenſual and brutiſh gratification, all thoſe fleſhly luſts which war againſt the ſoul, and prompt deluded ſinners to defile the temple of the living God—all thoſe baſe and ſpecious deceivers, which cry, " Peace, peace!" and there is no peace
" Joy,

"Joy, joy!" and there is no joy." Reject the brilliant imposture, which would array a spirit of darkness in the unsullied robes of an angel. Give no ear to the high swelling words of those, who, while they speak of liberty, are themselves the slaves of corruption. Dare these vain boasters assert—dare they imagine, that their life is, at any period, a life of pleasure? Ah, no! it is a life of wretchedness, of agony—of complicated, accumulated woe.

Dismissing indignantly such unfounded pretensions as these, let us investigate those objects of pursuit, which, as far as their nature will admit, put in their fair and reasonable claim to the title of happiness. Let us consider these innocent joys, which the Author of our being sends to sweeten the portion of life, to render that state to which he has called us estimable—joys which religion itself approves, warrants, recommends, fanc-

sanctifies. There is nothing in all these which controverts the proposition—there is every thing which confirms and establishes it, "that we have brighter joys in prospect." One argument, if argument be at all wanted, shall suffice, instead of a thousand, by way of demonstration. These earthly blessings are always attended by *anxiety* : anxiety, which rises in proportion to the ardour with which we enjoy them—anxiety, which is most keenly felt, when we are in the midst of all the fond endearments of life, when we are in possession of the world's best treasures. What is that joy, that it should absorb all our faculties, and engross the whole attachment of our souls, which, ere long, must necessarily flee away and depart; and which, in the mean time, we hold by such a precarious tenure, that soon—very soon—to-morrow perhaps—it may vanish, and be no more? Where are we, when thoughts like these obtrude themselves, as they must

SERM. XV.

must occasionally do, on the sickening heart? Verily every man living, at his best state, is altogether vanity. His happiness is little more than a splendid dream, from which the reality of sorrow must awaken him. If it be a treasure, it is a treasure lodged " in earthen vessels * ;" gold that soon becometh dim—fine gold that is soon changed. It is a flower of delicious fragrance—but oh how fragile! how transient! In the morning it is green and groweth up—in the evening it is cut down, dried up, and withered.

Enjoy then, but enjoy with chastened pleasure, the temporal felicity which God has bestowed upon you. Cherish this boon, as proceeding from the kind indulgence of Heaven; but affix not to it more importance than it deserves. The best blessings and enjoyments of which our mortal state is capable are trifling and of small estimation when

* 2 Cor. iv. 7.

The Promise of Christian Hope.

compared with that good and perfect gift, which cometh down from the Father of lights. *That* gift may also be yours, and that joy, which no time, no disasters, can take away from you.

Take heed, therefore, that ye build your habitation in the munition of the rocks: do not decorate too lavishly those structures which are lightly raised upon the sand. Remember the conditions on which you hold your state of being. "Set your affections on things above; not on things on the earth." Hold yourselves in readiness to depart, for this is not your rest.

II. Thus speaketh the divine monitor in the day of our joy, and in the day of the gladness of our heart. With what increased energies does the voice come home to our bosoms in the hour of *sorrow*, the season of tribulation and anguish, in the dark and cloudy day?

" when

"when we review the monuments of our withered joys, of our blasted hopes—if there be yet any monuments of them remaining, more than a mournful remembrance which they have left behind in our afflicted souls*? With what eagerness do we then cling to the thought that *this is not our rest*—a thought, which, perhaps, in the moment of our fancied pleasures, was a memento painful as was the hand-writing on the wall to the heart of the king of Babylon, when in the midst of his feasting and revelry he was struck with consternation, and all his songs were turned into mourning! Ah, let not them that are deceived trust in vanity—let them not frame to themselves fantastic hopes which never can be realized! Sorrows are necessary—they are certain—they are unavoidable. It is not more sure that man is born, than that he is born to trouble. Our fairest hopes are often frustrated—the projects

* Doddridge.

which we form with the utmoſt probability of ſucceſs frequently prove abortive, and leave us a prey to diſappointment. The ſources of comfort which once we fondly deemed inexhauſtible, vaniſh out of our ſight—as the ſtream of brooks they paſs away—they go to nothing, and periſh. Pretended friends deceive, betray, deſert us—and time diminiſhes the number (ſmall at its beſt!) of real ones. The Lord may write us childleſs: or he may ſlay the beloved fruit of the womb—or perhaps we may know what it is to have our love requited by hatred: our kindneſs by ingratitude; our fondeſt, tendereſt anxieties by obduracy and rebellion. Our fortunes may ſuffer ſhipwreck—poverty and want may come upon us—we may look in vain for a protecting hand to help us in our calamity. We may ſmart under the contumely of the ſcorner, or groan beneath the fury of the oppreſſor. Our native land may be viſited by the ſcourges of divine

divine wrath—famine may waſte, diſeaſe may annoy it; the alarm of war may ſound within its borders. We may ourſelves be enervated by pining ſickneſs, harraſſed and tortured by pain. Reaſon, that vicegerent of heaven, may be for a time diſturbed and driven from its ſeat. However many or however few of theſe calamities we may be called upon to ſuſtain, one ſtruggle at all events awaits us. Death, triumphant Death, marks us for his prey, and with a ſtern ſmile tells us, that we are duſt and aſhes.

When we are feeble and ſore ſmitten, and the hour of afflidtion taketh hold upon us—when our eyes are dim by reaſon of ſorrow, and we go mourning all the day long—at this ſeaſon to hear, as it were the voice of an angel, bidding us, "Ariſe and depart;" telling us, that our reſt is not here— fixing our thoughts on the regions of bliſs, and directing our eyes to the

ever-

everlasting hills—pointing out that cloudless heaven, whence fear and grief, and every species of misery, is for ever excluded—awakening us from the unreal visions of life to the contemplation of those joys which are perfect and eternal, and therefore perfect, *because* they are eternal—calling us to Jesus, the Mediator of a new covenant, the Author and Giver of Peace, who opens his everlasting arms to receive us, and says, " Come unto me, all ye that labour and are heavy laden, and I will give you rest"—this is indeed to taste and see how gracious the Lord is, and how blessed they, who put their trust in him. O the strong consolations of religion! O glorious prospect of immortality! Thou that art afflicted, and tossed with the tempest, fear not, for thy Saviour hath redeemed thee—he hath called thee by thy name—thou art his own. " When thou passest through the waters, he will be with thee; and through the rivers, they

SERM. XV.

they shall not overflow thee—when thou walkest through the fire, thou shalt not be burned, neither shall the flame kindle upon thee. "Take comfort, take com-"fort, O my people," saith your God.

While we meditate with fervent gratitude on declarations soothing and gracious as these—whilst we contrast the happiness of a future and eternal state of being with our temporal sorrows and sufferings, we are, for a season, carried "out of the body *." We dwell, with fond anticipation, on the hour of our departure. A blaze of such unutterable glory shines round about us, that, like the celebrated Convert, when we would open our eyes to the occurrences of life, we find that they have lost their perceptive powers. But He who points out to us these sublime aspirations, does at the same time direct

* 2 Cor. xii. 2, 3.

and

and regulate their ardours. It is good for a man, that his treasure, and his heart, be in heaven—but it is good also that he tarry the Lord's leisure, and trust submissively to the dispensation of His wise Providence. "All the days of my "appointed time," said the great exemplar of patience, "all the days of my "appointed time will I wait, till my "change come."

But admonitions of a far different kind are perhaps more frequently necessary. Too often, when our minds are oppressed with sorrow, Faith, the guardian of the soul, sinks into a lethargic kind of slumber, and Sin, coming hand in hand, with Misery, casts deadly ingredients into the medicinal cup, which was prepared for us to drink. While we feel, by sad experience, that "this is not our rest," we forget, what it is of the utmost consequence we should remember, that there *remaineth* a rest for the people of God.

SERM.
XV.

God. And can we then be ignorant of the proper object of our hopes and desires? Can we sink under the pressure of sorrow, when we might aspire after, and prepare ourselves for, the felicity of saints, the society of angels, the presence of God? Can we suffer our thoughts to abide prostrate on the earth, when they might take wing, and fly up to heaven? Why should we abandon ourselves to despondency, when the God of hope would fill us with joy and peace in believing? Why should we suffer our whole attention to be engrossed by the sorrows and anxieties of a perishable world? Why should we not cherish the blessings vouchsafed to us, perform the duties enjoined by our gracious Master, and look for permanent happiness to that blessed country whither we are going?

O let us fear, my beloved brethren, lest, a promise being left us of entering into that

that rest, any of us, through carelessness or unbelief, should come short of it. Let us hold fast our profession without wavering. Let us place our confidence and our reliance on the promises of God. Above all, let us not, by our own wilful depravity, cancel the precious privileges of redemption, nor abandon our inestimable hope, for the horrible defilements of sin. When the bright prospect of immortal glory is presented to our view, shall we choose death rather than life, and desperately plunge ourselves into the abyss of sensuality? Shall we, O shame! lie grovelling amidst the pollutions of Egypt, and taste its unhallowed meats, when we might partake of the celestial manna, and be fed with angel's food? Shall we obstinately linger in this waste howling wilderness, wherein are serpents and scorpions, and drought; suffering the river of God, which is full of water, to flow, untasted and unheeded, by us; and despising the land of promise, our heavenly

SERM. XV.

heavenly inheritance? If such is our fatal depravity, let us at least open our eyes to its consequences—let us remember, that the message of God, by his prophet, instead of awakening comfort in the bosom, will to us be a message of lamentation, and mourning, and woe! O terrible voice of most just judgement, when to the call, "*Arise, and depart*," shall be annexed this tremendous sentence, that doom of the enemies of God, ARISE ye, to receive your Father's curse—DEPART, from the presence of the Almighty. Look not towards the bright mansions of immortal glory. This is not *your* rest. The wicked shall be turned into hell, and all the people that forget God.

Does the heart of the sinner tremble within him? Is he appalled by a sense of conscious guilt, and by the terrors of the wrath of God? Let him seek the face of him from whom he hath deeply revolted

revolted—let him turn unto the Lord, and he will have mercy upon him, and to our God, for he will abundantly pardon. Let him trust to the atonement made by Christ, to the blood of that immaculate Lamb who was slain to be the propitiation for our sins. To-day, even now, hear his voice, and harden not your hearts. For thus speaketh the word of Eternal Mercy—thus speaketh He, who once came to save, and who will hereafter come to judge, the world:

" Arise ye, and depart from the death
" of sin, unto the life of righteousness!
" Repent, and turn yourselves from all
" your transgressions, so iniquity shall
" not be your ruin. Cast away from
" you all your transgressions whereby
" ye have transgressed, and make you a
" new heart and a new spirit. I have
" no pleasure in the death of him that
" dieth, saith the Lord God: wherefore
" turn yourselves, and live ye!"

He

The Promise of Christian Hope.

He which teftifieth thefe things faith, Surely I come quickly. Amen."

EVEN SO COME, LORD JESUS!

SERMON

SERMON XVI.

THE CHRISTIAN'S WARFARE.

Y SERMON

SERMON XVI.

THE CHRISTIAN'S WARFARE.

JOB i.—6, 7.

Now there was a day, when the sons of God came to present themselves before the Lord, and Satan came also among them.

And the Lord said unto Satan, "Whence "comest thou?" Then Satan answered the Lord, and said, " FROM GOING TO AND FRO IN THE EARTH, AND FROM WALKING UP AND DOWN IN IT."

WITH what impressions of reverential awe does the soul (borne on the wings of inspiration), see visions of high mystery, when we are introduced as it were into the courts of Heaven, and participate in the counsels of God!

But when we behold that great and dreadful Adversary, whose delight is in our misery, whose object is our irretrievable ruin—when we behold *him* admitted into the presence of Jehovah, fearfulness and trembling taketh hold of us, and an horrible dread is ready to overwhelm us. Having no power of ourselves to help ourselves, no means whereby we may oppose or counteract the devices of the enemy, we should give up all for lost—the cloud of eternal woe would burst over us—could we not run, as to a strong tower, to the protection of our God. If God be for us, even Satan cannot prevail against us. He may assault our faith—he may make trial of our virtue—but the Almighty will not leave us in his hand: the Lord will

will not utterly fail his people, nor forsake his inheritance. Thou, O blessed Jesus, art our refuge—thou alone art the strength of our confidence *The very devils are subject unto us through thy name.* They know thee, who thou art, O thou Holy One of God, and they tremble at thy power. Protected by thine omnipotent arm, we shall quench all the fiery darts of the wicked. Thy voice will speak comfortably unto us, as it did to thy chosen disciples: " Behold, I give " you power to tread on serpents and " scorpions, and on all the power of " the enemy; and nothing shall by any " means hurt you."

But be it remembered, that it is only the aid of God that we can conquer. Were we left to our own insufficient powers, the Destroyer would find us an easy prey; the Son of wickedness would triumph in our overthrow. What then have not they to fear, who, instead of flying

SERM. XVI.

to the Almighty for support against the enemy of their eternal peace, add rebellion to their sin—become confederates with the powers of darkness, and lift up their voices against God? What horrors are presented to our view, when this tremendous agency is employed for the judicial punishment of guilt—when Satan himself becomes an instrument in the hand of a just God to pour down vengeance and fury on the impenitent! "I saw the Lord," saith the intrepid prophet*, " I saw the Lord sitting on his throne, and all the host of heaven standing by him, on his right hand and on his left. And the Lord said, " Who shall persuade Ahab, that he may go up and fall at Ramoth Gilead?" And one said on this manner, and another said on that manner. And there came forth a spirit, and stood before the Lord, and said, " I will persuade him—for I will " be a lying spirit in the mouth of all his

* 1 Kings xxii. 19.

" pro-

prophets." You are no strangers to the event. It was such as might be expected, where the Author of evil, instead of being restrained from his purposes by the Almighty, was empowered, was *commissioned,* to destroy. Ahab hearkened to the servants of Baal—he despised the true prophet—he set at nought the counsel of God. For this cause God sent him a strong delusion that he might believe a lie: and he, who had often shed man's blood, became subject to the law of eternal justice, and by man his blood was shed.

The fact then is certain, and incontrovertible, that there is, in the unseen world (the existence of which no one doubts, who has either the faith of a christian, or the common sense of a man) a restless, active, malignant Spirit*.

* See Wilberforce, § II. 2.

And

And it is no lefs certain, that this malignant Spirit is permitted to direct his weapons of warfare, fundry and manifold as they are, againft mankind: but in the exercife of this power he is under the fupreme controul of Almighty God.

The word "Satan" in its' original fenfe fignifies *an accufer*. It is of the fame meaning and import with the Greek term, from which we call our fpiritual Adverfary "the Devil;" whom the infpired Apoftle and Evangelift defcribes under the name of "the *Accufer* of the brethren, which accufeth them before our God day and night." In that portion of facred hiftory which I am now fubmitting to your confideration, we behold him in the immediate difcharge of his office. Envious at the felicity of an holy and blamelefs faint of God, he forms a project to overturn that felicity—to caft the patriarch into the

the furnace of affliction, in hopes that by this means the gold might lose a part of its lustre—that the perfect and upright man might fall from his stedfastness, and sin against God—that, overcome by the severity of his sufferings, the candidate for immortality might be disappointed of his most precious hope.

To this day, to this hour, the object of our enemy is the same. Still does he seek to deprive mankind of the favour of God, and to blot their names out of the book of life. To this end, he is to the righteous a spirit of *arrogance* and *presumption*; raising them to the giddy elevations of pharisaical pride, that he may cast them down headlong. To the inconstant and wavering he is a spirit of *doubt* and *perplexity*; at his suggestions, scruples and difficulties bewilder their thoughts, and stumbling-blocks are set for them in every path. To the worldly-minded he is a spirit of eager and insatiable

tiable *defire*, eftranging them from their better hope by the riches and pleafures of this vain life. To the timid and fainthearted he is a fpirit of *terror* and *alarm*. He reprefents the Almighty, not as the Father of mercies, not as the Friend and Preferver of men, but as merely an avenger to execute wrath—an hard and auftere mafter, a cruel and revengeful tyrant, the foe to human happinefs. To the fallen he is a fpirit of *defpair*. He cafts a dark and gloomy veil over their eyes, concealing from their view, as much as poffible, the tender mercies of God our Saviour, who would not that any fhould perifh ; but that all fhould come to repentance. As the holy apoftle was in things pertaining to godlinefs, fo is Satan in works of a malicious tendency: " He is all things to all men, that he may by all means gain fome." And having fucceeded in his wily ftratagems, having caufed the finner to fall by that fin which did moft eafily befet him—

when

when man has listened to the pestilent arts of the great Seducer, and has perished in his transgression—the evil spirit will hereafter be ready, with malignant alacrity, to execute those judgments which await the impenitent offender. He, who was the means of bringing sinners to the place of torment, will then be the instrument of inflicting on them the vengeance of that God whom they renounced, provoked, and blasphemed.

This power of Satan, his hatred to mankind, his incessant and cruel activity, gave rise to that solemn injunction delivered by the holy apostle with so much earnestness to his converts: " Be " sober," saith he, " be vigilant; because " your adversary the devil, as a roaring " lion, walketh about, seeking whom he " may devour: *whom resist, stedfast in* " *the faith.*"

Why

SERM. XVI.

Why this principle of evil is permitted by Heaven to exist, and why mankind are under its dreadful influence, is a mystery known only unto God. We dare not, we cannot, investigate it. We adore in humble submission that all-gracious Providence, which, while the danger is near us, points out the remedy—bids us be resolute in the contest; and tells us what will be the fearful doom of those who suffer themselves to be vanquished by the enemy of their souls. "The "same shall drink of the wine of the "wrath of God, which is poured out "without measure into the cup of his "indignation; and they shall have no "rest day nor night; but the smoke of "their torment shall ascend up for ever "and ever." On the contrary, if we follow the example of our Saviour Christ—if, like him, we rebuke the malignant spirit, saying. " Get thee hence, Satan! I will wor- "ship the Lord my God, and Him only "will I serve," then we are assured that the

the devil will leave us; and that in his stead angels shall come and minister unto us.

Of the history of the immaterial world we know no more than the Spirit of God hath been pleased to reveal. For further information we must wait with patience till that hour, which shall bring to light the hidden things of darkness, and shall make manifest the counsels of eternal wisdom. In the mean time we are given to understand, that among the angels, created by God, there were some who daringly rebelled against the supreme power of Jehovah. *There was war in Heaven.* The Almighty, in his just indignation, punished the offending spirits for their presumption; dismissed them for ever from the habitations of his holiness and of his glory, and consigned them to those regions of woe, where the worm dieth not, and the fire is not quenched. When man was created in the image of God, was placed

placed in Paradise, and was in a state of preparation for future glories of a more exalted nature, then we are told, that " through envy of the devil sin entered into the world." The tempter then began, and pursued with fatal success, his work of destruction. In direct opposition and defiance to the behests of heaven, our first parents listened to the specious promises of the seducer. They fell, and the ruin was great; for with them fell a world. Then was the curse poured upon them and upon their children, the wretched heirs of transgression and sorrow. And we should have remained in a state of condemnation, without the possibility of recovery, had not the Son of God, in the fulness of time, by his death destroyed him that had the power of death, even the devil, and by his resurrection restored to mortals the hope of everlasting life.

Having

Having confidered the inveterate enmity of Satan, and its dreadful confequences, we find ourfelves at a lofs for words in which to exprefs our aftonifhment and concern, that this great object of a mortal's fear and deteftation, this mighty and revengeful fpirit, full of all malice and hatred, who is fuffered by God to wage war againft the bodies and fouls of men, to caufe prefent mifery, and to inflict future punifhment—that this author of fpiritual and temporal evil fhould gain fuch an afcendancy over the minds of unhappy mortals, that they both think and fpeak lightly of eternal woe; diveft themfelves of thofe fenfations of horror which they ought ever to entertain on a fubject fo tremendous, and are even fo infatuated as to make a mock at fin and mifery—nay, to connect ideas of frantic jefting with the name of the enemy of their fouls—with a fubject of all others the moft awful and alarming!

In some cases indeed the adversary proceeds still further; and contrives to persuade the poor deluded sinner that he may walk in safety along the path of transgression, assuring him, that there is no truth in what has been asserted of the existence of an evil spirit, or of a place of future torment: that these are the dreams of superstition — the idle chimeras of enthusiasm—old and exploded fables, fit to terrify weak and bigotted minds, but unworthy of any reception among the philosophic and the wise. This is one of the most artful of all the stratagems of Satan. When the heart of man is once lulled to sleep by the opiate of unbelief, all is easy. No stings of conscience remain, no tortures of self-reproach, no fear, no salutary remorse. The wretched offender plunges without scruple into all the excesses of guilt—he follows the propensities of his corrupt mind, and considers not that for all these things God will bring him

him into judgment. Thus the subtle poison, disguised by careful concealment, penetrates unsuspected into the veins, and drinketh up the spirit to its destruction.

My brethren, you are not ignorant of the devices of your adversary. It is your bounden duty to guard with unremitting vigilance every inlet of your hearts. Suspect yourselves. Examine carefully into the state of your souls. Look well if there be any way of wickedness in you—any unhallowed inmate lurking in your bosoms: for the malignant enemy, who in the days of our forefathers walked to and fro in the earth, still continues to pursue us with unabated fury. He faints not, neither is he weary in evil-doing. He was a deceiver from the beginning of time: he will continue to deceive, till the earth is razed from its fondations. As he said to the first victims of his treachery,

SERM.
XVI.

chery, so saith he to us all in the hour of temptation, "Ye shall not die." But what saith the Almighty? "The "soul that sinneth, it *shall* die." How often are the declarations of heavenly truth disregarded! How often are the lying oracles of Satan listened to with avidity! Whenever your perverse inclinations lead you to evil, be assured that you are the immediate objects of his accursed designs. When you go astray in the paths of intemperance and uncleanness—when you are carried away by the violence of your angry passions, and your too ready tongue gives utterance to curses and execrations—when you deceive, and slander, and defraud, and betray—when you oppress and persecute your neighbour—when in any instance you transgress the laws of the Almighty—when you profane the sacred rest of the Sabbath of God, and neglect to assemble yourselves together in the place where his honour dwelleth—when you

you wilfully abstain from the Lord's table, and separate yourselves from your brethren, who come to feed on the banquet of that heavenly food—in all, or in any of these instances of depravity, your souls are as surely under the influence of the evil spirit, as was the body of the poor dæmoniac in the gospel, who wandered on the mountains or amongst the tombs, naked, bleeding, frantic, desperate, crying, and cutting himself with stones.

But there is yet another method, whereby the enemy of mankind beguiles unstable souls to their destruction. I mean, the fatal artifice, which gives fond and flattering names to notorious vices; thereby confounding the distinctions between good and evil, and divesting mankind of the horror which they ought to entertain at the violation of their duty to God. The diabolical and most unchristian spirit of anger and revenge, which terminates in bloodshed and murder, and sends many a wretched soul, unprepared, into the presence of an offended God, is disguised with the high-sounding title of *honour*. The base and infamous violation of the dearest ties by which human society is holden, ties which the Author of our being consecrates with his blessing, and on which all domestic happiness depends — this atrocious wickedness is distinguished by the name of *gallantry:* and the criminal, instead of meeting with discouragement and reprobation from the world, partakes as largely of its smiles and its favour, as if he were a pattern of every social virtue. That thoughtless and fatal dissipation, which consigns to poverty and distress the gamester's innocent family—that extravagance, which, not content with simple ruin, entails complicated misery on all those with whom the libertine is connected, is termed a system of *spirit*, and *gaiety*. And that gloomy

gloomy infidelity, which tends to rob us of our heavenly treasure, and to do away our hope of redemption through a Saviour's atonement (that hope, without which life is a burden, and death an infupportable torment), is by the ufages of a corrupt world celebrated as the perfection of *wifdom*, *liberality*, and *philofophy*. With fuch fatal fuccefs doth the Tempter go to and fro in the earth—fo triumphantly walketh he up and down in it!

The wiles of Satan are infinite in their number; his power is great and very terrible: but the Chriftian muft not therefore confider his own fituation as defperate. He cannot be ignorant, that there is an omnipotent arm, able to check the mighty foe in the midft of his career, and to deliver the prey from his rapacity. In the holy book from whence my text is taken, we have a proof of that fupreme controul, by which

which the adversary is limited in the execution of his purposes. " Hitherto shalt thou come," saith the voice of God, " and no further"—here shall thy pride and thy malignity be stayed. *On himself lay not thine hand!* and afterwards, *Touch not his life.* The mysteries of the invisible world are as yet hidden from our eyes; but, while we are beset by many spiritual dangers, we rejoice in a sense of the divine protection, and of the ministry of those celestial guardians, who, unknown and unseen, watch over us for our good. When an host of men encamped against Elisha, and the heart of his attendant was filled with terror and apprehension, the prophet had recourse to his God. The prayer of faith opened the eyes of the young man: he beheld, and, lo! the mountain on which he stood was covered with horses and chariots of fire, and the heavenly host was seen, forming an invincible rampart around his master. As it was

was in the days of Elisha, so is it now; so shall it be also, even unto the end of the world. Fear not therefore, O Christian! Thou that puttest thy trust in the Lord, fear not! They that are *for* us are more, and mightier, than those which are *against* us.

Yet must we be aware, that the guardianship of Angels will not afford us protection, if we are deficient in our own exertions. Ours is a warfare, a combat, on which more than our existence depends; in its event still dearer interests are involved. Eternal life is the high prize of our victory. That we may obtain it, we must wrestle against the principalities and powers of darkness—we must remember, that " no man that warreth entangleth himself with the affairs of this life"—we must contend against spiritual wickedness—we must be sober and vigilant—we must put on the whole armour of God.

SERM. XVI.

In this state of inceffant hoftility with the powers of darkness, we must look unto the Author and Finisher of our faith, the Captain of our falvation. He was the promifed "feed of the woman" who, by bruifing the ferpent's head, fhould bring redemption unto a fallen world. To effect this work of mercy, he difdained not to quit for a feafon the throne of his glory. By his holy miniftry, by his amazing miracles, the power of Satan was overthrown. Armed with the facred oracles of God, the blessed Jefus triumphed glorioufly; and He who was himfelf tempted, is able to fuccour them that are tempted. Through Him we fhall do great acts; it is He that fhall tread down our enemies. "For this purpofe the Son of God was manifefted, THAT HE MIGHT DESTROY THE WORKS OF THE DEVIL."

SERMON

SERMON XVII.

THE CHRISTIAN'S DEFENCE.

SERMON XVII.

THE CHRISTIAN'S DEFENCE.

PSALM xci. 2.

I will say of the Lord, " He is my refuge, " and my fortress—my God—in Him will " I trust."

WHEN the apostles, alarmed by the surrounding tempest, hastily awoke their Lord from that tranquil sleep in which they beheld him, the Saviour of mankind first demonstrated his sovereign

vereign power over the elements by appeasing the storm, and then gently rebuked his too timid followers : " Why " are ye so fearful ? *How is it that ye* " *have no faith ?*"

When, in another instance, the impatient zeal of Simon Peter had led him to an enterprize of the most imminent danger, and he assayed to walk upon the pathless waves, that he might meet his Lord, Jesus put forth his hand, and caught him as he was sinking into the abyss of waters, adding these remarkable words, " *O thou of little faith*, wherefore " didst thou doubt?"

From these two signal examples, and from many others which might be adduced, it appears, that we are more apt to be afraid, in proportion as we are less disposed to believe—that fear is a betraying of the succours which *Religion*, as well as *Reason*, offereth—and that a

sense

sense of the divine protection is the strongest support we can experience in the trials and temptations of this precarious world.

The Courage, therefore, which it inspires, is among the best privileges which Christianity confers upon us, as it tends to remove those terrors which are without foundation, and to sustain us, when we are encompassed by real danger. "When I am weak, then am I strong. "I can do all things, through Christ, "which strengthens me. I will say of "the Lord, *He is my hope, and my strong* "*hold*—my God—*in him will I trust.*" Such is the language of faith upon all occasions where the Christian is called on for the exertion of his fortitude. That fortitude does not consist in noisy and boisterous expressions of fearlessness, which are far from unequivocal proofs of true courage; it does not consist in rashly defying all that can possibly happen

pen of a dangerous nature: but it is cool, moderate, and unaffuming; not apt to fink into defpondency, or to fwell with prefumption; and thus, infpiring the believer with fentiments worthy of the hope fet before him, it bears undeniable teftimony to the excellence, the divinity of its origin.

Bleffed is he who hath the God of Jacob for his help, and whofe truft is in the Lord his God. While we reft under his defence, we may be affured, that, without his efpecial permiffion, no evil fhall happen to us, nor fhall any plague (but for our ultimate good) come nigh our dwelling. We fhall abide under the fhadow of the Almighty. We fhall be fecure under the covert of his wings. He will give his angels charge over us, to keep us in all our ways.

Thus fheltered, thus defended, we fhall not be afraid for any terror by night,

night, nor for the arrow that flieth by day. We shall commit ourselves chearfully to the divine protection; assuredly trusting, that through the day we shall be preserved from danger; and that, when we lay us down in peace to take our rest, no enemy shall be suffered to interrupt our repose. The good Shepherd neither slumbereth nor sleepeth. He " keepeth watch over his flock by " night."

But the eye of the Lord is in every place; he beholdeth the evil as well as the good. His omniscience penetrates into the counsels of the wicked—there is no darkness nor shadow of death where they can hide themselves from his all-pervading knowlege. Whither can they go from his spirit, or whither can they flee from his presence? If they say in their hearts " Who seeth us? we are compassed about with darkness— what need have we to fear?" These men know not that the eyes of the Lord

are

are ten thoufand times brighter than the fun, beholding all the ways of man, and confidering the moft fecret paths*. Nay, if the myfterious purpofe of evil is confined to one bofom, if no lip has revealed the fecret mifchief, yet the Almighty, who knows what is in man, can bring to light the hidden things of darknefs, and punifh with open infamy what has been devifed with cautious fecrefy. God fcattereth the proud in the imagination of their hearts. He that dwelleth in heaven fhall laugh them to fcorn—the Lord fhall have them in derifion. Hence it is, that the wicked flee when no man purfueth—while the righteous is bold as a lion. Take a remarkable inftance of pious intrepidity, as recorded in the hiftory of holy Nehemiah. He was employed in a moft important work; even that of rebuilding the city of Jerufalem, and reftoring the worfhip of the true God. This labour

* Ecclefiafticus xxiii. 18, 19.

of love, performed with the moſt zealous diligence, raiſed againſt him divers malicious enemies, who by every means in their power ſought his deſtruction. A falſe and treacherous prophet, approaching him while yet his work was unaccompliſhed, endeavoured to ſhake his conſtancy by communicating intelligence of the moſt alarming nature. "Let us meet together," ſaith he, "in the houſe of God within the temple, and let us ſhut the doors of the temple; for they will come to ſlay thee: yea, in the night will they come to ſlay thee." This meſſage would have filled a weak and timid heart with conſternation; and would have tempted one leſs ſtrong in the faith to have abandoned the taſk of public duty in which he was engaged, that he might conſult his individual ſafety. But the holy man, whoſe refuge and fortreſs was God, undauntedly replied, "Should ſuch a man as I flee? And who is there, that, being as I am, would

would enter into the temple to save his life? I will not go in." And lo, saith Nehemiah, "I perceived that God had not sent him, but that he pronounced this prophecy against me; for Sanballat and Tobiah had hired him. Therefore was he hired, that I should be afraid, and do so, and sin, and that they might have matter against me for an evil report, that they might reproach me." Had a message of a similar nature been received by his wicked and dastardly enemies, it would, in all probability, have had a very different effect. No bolts would have been deemed sufficiently secure, no guard sufficiently strong, to defend their worthless persons from the threatened danger.

I am far from wishing to insinuate, that a sense of the divine protection should make us neglect the care necessary for our personal safety. We are not to sit down in torpid inactivity, presuming

ing on affiftance from above. The watchman muft be faithful and vigilant, though we know that, except the Lord keepeth the city, he waketh but in vain. It is no more improper to provide for our own fecurity in cafes of danger, becaufe God is able to protect us, than it is culpable to procure the means of fuftenance for our families, becaufe God could at his pleafure open the windows of heaven, and pour down plenty upon us, or could feed us by miracle, as he fed his prophet Elijah, or the children of Ifrael in the wildernefs. He hath commanded us to take all meafures conducive to our prefervation, which are not inconfiftent with the precepts of his gofpel. It then remains for Him to crown thofe meafures with fuccefs. Without his aid all our exertions muft be ineffectual. We are to do the utmoft in our power, in full reliance on his mercy; and are then to caft all our care upon God, knowing that he careth for us.

SERM. XVII.

When a company of malicious Jews bound themselves by an horrible oath, that they would neither eat nor drink till they had slain the apostle of God, the watchful care of Divine Providence disappointed their dark and murderous design. It became known (how, we enquire not) to those who were nearly interested in the welfare of St. Paul, and who immediately conveyed to him the alarming intelligence. Observe the steps taken in consequence of this, by the servant of God. He doth not dismiss the informant with a contemptuous smile, as defying all that his enemies could devise or perpetrate against him, and resting his defence on God alone. He was aware that this would have been presumption, and not piety. Knowing that his life was of the utmost importance to the cause of truth, he immediately prepares for his safety—he procures a guard to accompany him in his flight, and is conveyed, under the wings of the Roman Eagle,

Eagle, from Jerusalem to Cæsarea. A stronger instance can hardly be adduced of the propriety, the necessity, the duty of self-defence, and the obligation we are under to preserve, by every means in our power, that life which God hath given us for the promotion of his glory.

But, while we take this necessary care, we are to rely entirely on our heavenly Father for that blessing, on which all our exertions must ultimately depend for success. The power which imparted life, alone can preserve it. God is the Lord, by whom we escape death. In him therefore let us put our trust—and, when we are rescued from danger, let us not assume to ourselves any merit, as though by our own power or holiness we had averted the impending calamity—but, being strong in the faith, let us give glory to God. How, indeed, can we arrogate to ourselves any degree of merit? We are weak and short-sighted

—we see but a small portion of those evils which surround us—in many cases we perceive neither the danger nor the deliverance. In a word, all good proceeds from God; and no evil can happen without his permission.

Thus, when Jesus stood before the Roman Governor, and, feeling all the conscious dignity of innocence, for a while opened not his sacred lips, Pilate cried out, " Speakest thou not unto me? " Knowest thou not, that I have power " to crucify thee, and have power to " release thee?" Jesus at length answered, " *Thou couldst have no power at* " *all against me, except it were given thee* " *from above.*" In the exercise of that delegated power we see at the first view only oppressed, injured, bleeding innocence—but, on more minute investigation, we find that thus the salvation of a world was effected—that our ransom was paid—that our iniquities were pardoned.

doned. We behold the sufferings of the man Christ Jesus doing away the sin of many—and the malice, even of hell itself, made subservient to the purposes of divine mercy. The eternal Son of God was made a curse for us, that he might redeem us from the curse of the law, and translate us to the blessings of his heavenly kingdom.

To foresee the end from the beginning —to understand at one view the vast series of events, whereby all things, however apparently evil, will ultimately produce and work out universal good— this is the prerogative of Omniscience alone. Such knowlege is too wonderful and excellent for man—he cannot attain unto it. Here the christian must not count himself to have apprehended [*]; but this one thing he may do. Dismissing all corrosive anxiety, and hush-

---

[*] See Philippians iii.—13.

ing all the tumults of the foul to peace, he may fay of the Lord, "HE IS MY GOD." The form is brief and fimple—but in the privilege to which it refers, what bleffings are comprifed! In that one word of mighty efficacy, what hope, what comfort, what joy is included! While with reverence and admiration we contemplate the perfections of God, with tranfport unutterable we feel our own happy intereft in them all. While we dwell on that name, which is great, wonderful, and holy, we remember with delight that as his majefty is, fo is his mercy. While with hearts poffeffed by reverential awe we meditate on the divine attributes, we apply their glorious influence to ourfelves—we honour him, as he is God—we rejoice and are glad in him, as he is OUR God. In this relation we view in him all that the imagination can conceive or the foul defire of perfect good—all that zeal cherifhes, or religion adores—all that faith

faith promises, that hope expects, that love can realize. We not only behold almighty power, but we behold that power ever ready to protect and guard us—not only consummate wisdom, but that wisdom ever ready to teach and enlighten us—not only unbounded goodness, but that goodness ever ready to befriend and save us. As long as the Christian can address the Author of all grace by this dear and sacred appellation—as long as he can say unto the Lord " Thou art my God," he feels that his deliverance is completed, that his pardon is sealed, that his joys are hallowed, that his sorrows are assuaged, that his wants are supplied, that his cry is heard, that his person is accepted, that his prayers are answered, and that his praise ascends to Heaven. " I will say of the Lord, *He is my refuge and my fortress—* MY GOD—*in him will I trust.*"

And

SERM. XVII.

And can we then think too highly, my beloved brethren, of that transcendent mercy, whereby we are enabled to come boldly to the throne of grace, and to make our boast that God is our Father? There was a time, in the early ages of Christianity, when the disciples and converts were not permitted to use that prayer in which our Saviour teaches us to address the Almighty as a Parent, till they had passed through a time of previous discipline and probation *. It was deemed a privilege of too high import for those whose minds were not well informed in christian knowlege, and in the word of eternal life. It was reserved for them, till, being thoroughly ac-

* See this fact stated in Bingham's " Origines Ecclesiasticæ," Book I. Chap. 4. § 7.—where the learned author, in support of his assertion, appeals to the testimony of St. Chrysostom †, St. Augustin ‡, Theodoret §, and others. Hence the Lord's Prayer was called εὐχὴ πιστῶν, *The Prayer of Believers.*

† Chrysost. Hom. 2. in 2 Cor.
‡ Aug. Hom. 29. de Verb. Apost.
§ Theodor. Epit. Div. Dogm. c. 24.

quainted

quainted with the principles of the doctrine of Chrift, they were judged worthy to pafs on unto perfection. Then, received into the full communion of faints, and permitted to join in prayer with their holy brethren, they confidered themfelves as having gained admittance into the more immediate prefence of God; as being counted among the number of his children. They prefented themfelves in the fanctuary of God, as heirs of the covenant of mercy, and with joy unfpeakable and full of glory they exultingly cried out, "OUR FATHER, "*which art in heaven!*"

But can we prefume to call the omnipotent Lord of Heaven by the endearing titles of our Father and our God, if we dare to rebel againft him, and to provoke him by our difobedience? No. As long as we continue in fin, we muft expect, not his patronage and favour, but, what we juftly deferve, his fevere dif-

SERM. XVII.

displeasure. This displeasure is often mercifully shewn in lesser instances, before it proceeds to greater and more alarming judgments. And when we suffer aught, it is the consequence of our own offences, not of his want of power, or of goodness. " Behold, the Lord's " hand is not shortened that it cannot " save, neither his ear heavy that it *can-* " *not* hear; but your iniquities have " separated between you and your God, " and your sins have hid his face from " you, that he *will not* hear." O let us labour to have such an interest with our God, that we may enjoy all the benefit, all the high privilege of his Fatherly care! Let us lift up our hearts with our hands unto God in the heavens, and implore such a measure of his grace, that we may serve him acceptably, and, as far as is permitted to weak and imperfect mortals, may deserve his blessed protection!

In

In the mean time, as he " declareth " his almighty power moſt chiefly in " ſhewing mercy and pity," let us truſt implicitly in Him, and reſign ourſelves entirely to his divine Providence. Let a ſenſe of his goodneſs to us create ſuch love towards him, as may be at once the effect of paſt mercies, and the cauſe of future. " *Becauſe* he hath ſet his " love upon me," ſaith God of his ſervant, " therefore will I deliver him— " I will ſet him up, becauſe he hath " known my name."

For the watchful eye of Heaven, which looketh on all, looketh with peculiar favour and loving-kindneſs on thoſe who think on the Lord with a good heart, and in ſimplicity of heart ſeek him. He will be found of them that tempt him not, and he ſheweth himſelf unto ſuch as do not diſtruſt him*. Various are the terrors of the night; and manifold are the perils of the day; but the Chriſtian

* Wiſd. i. 1, 2.

SERM. XVII.

is under the protection of his God. He faith unto the Lord, " Thou art my re-
" fuge and my fortrefs—my God—in
" thee will I truſt. I will love thee, O
" Lord, my ſtrength—the Lord is my
" ſtrong rock and my defence, my Sa-
" viour, my GOD, and my might, my
" buckler, the horn alfo of my falvation,
" and my high tower."

I ſhall leave upon your minds the words of the bleſſed Pfalmiſt, who in the circumſtances of his various life, exemplified (perhaps beyond all other mortals) the fuperintending Providence of God, and the bleſſing of his heavenly fuccour:

" The Lord is my light and my fal-
" vation—whom then ſhall I fear? The
" Lord is the ſtrength of my life—of
" whom then ſhall I be afraid? When
" the wicked, even mine enemies and
" my foes, came againſt me to eat up
" my

" my flesh, they stumbled, and fell.
" Though an host of men were laid against
" me, yet shall not my heart be afraid;
" and though there rose up war against
" me, yet will I put my trust in Him. For
" in the time of trouble he shall hide me
" in his pavilion—in the secret place of
" his dwelling shall he hide me, and set
" me up upon a rock of stone. There-
" fore will I offer in his tabernacle an
" oblation of great joy; I will sing, yea,
" I will sing praises unto the Lord!"

SERMON

SERMON XVIII.

THE CHRISTIAN'S JOY.

SERMON XVIII.

THE CHRISTIAN'S JOY.

MATTHEW xiv.—27.

" *Be of good cheer—it is I—be not
" afraid!*"

NEVER was that gracious voice uttered, but for the benefit, the comfort, the inftruction of its hearers. In all fituations and circumftances of life, but more efpecially in cafes of perplexity, of danger, of forrow, the words of Chrift

bring

bring joy, and confolation, and hope, and peace.

The unbounded love of our compaffionate Saviour led him to weep for his perfecutors—to pray for his murderers. Can we wonder then, that in a peculiar manner he was interefted for thofe whom he was wont to diftinguifh by the endearing appellation of " friends" and " brethren?" that in all their affliction he was afflicted? that the Angel of his prefence faved them? that in his love and in his pity he redeemed them? that he bare them, and carried them all the days of old?

The words of my text reprefent the Saviour of mankind, in the fulnefs of his tranfcendent mercy, addreffing his difciples, when the fea wrought and was tempeftuous againft them, when their hearts melted away becaufe of the trouble. Their Lord had left them for a feafon,

a season, while, in mysterious retirement, he communed with the Eternal Father. It was night: the disciples were on the sea alone: and their ship, tossed with the violence of the storm, (which carried them as it were to heaven, and down again to the deep) was threatened with immediate destruction. In this forlorn and disconsolate situation they behold one " travelling in the greatness of his strength" on the mighty waters—miraculously changing the nature of the elements, and causing the liquid surface of the sea to become a firm pavement for his feet.

As he advanced, new fear was added to their former terrors. The strangeness of the sight—the time of its appearance, (which increased their superstitious alarms, and impressed on their minds the idea that unembodied spirits were then roaming about the world)—their own helpless and miserable situation—all thefe combined horrors made them infenfible to the bleffing which awaited them. Their eyes were holden: they did not know their Saviour. Inftead therefore of being welcomed by the acclamations of grateful tranfport, he was received by a fhriek of confternation. But how foon was their forrow turned into joy, their fear into fongs of deliverance, when they recognized their beloved Mafter — when they faw him haftening to fave them—when they heard his divine and confolatory voice, "Be " of good cheer—it is I—be not afraid!"

Not to his difciples only does our Lord addrefs himfelf. He fpeaks to all who believe on him through their word—to every child of his adoption—to every heir of his glorious promifes. When he approaches, mercy, ftrength, falvation, and bleffings innumerable accompany him. His prefence revives the heart: his comforts refrefh the foul. We are

are delivered from our adverfity, or we are enabled patiently to bear it. Our light afflictions are but for a moment. They are fucceeded by an eternal weight of glory.

In the feafon of darknefs and gloominefs, a conftant fenfe of our Lord's prefence and protection is our only fource of confidence. His word alone is a lamp unto our feet, and a light unto our paths. But if we forfake this unerring Guide, if we clofe our eyes againft the truth, if our ears are dull of hearing, if our hearts are hardened, we have then no refuge againft the ftorm. What marvel, if the floods run over us?—if we fink, as lead, in the mighty waters?

Whatever be our lot, whatever our condition here below, let us caft our care upon our Redeemer, and rely, with ftedfaft confidence, on his power and mercy: then fhall we fee him ready at hand

hand to help and to befriend us. Then shall we hear his all-gracious voice exhorting us to be of good cheer—bidding us lift up our heads with joy—telling us to banish all terror and apprehension. "*It is I—be not afraid.* It is I, your Saviour, your Protector, your Comforter." Blessed tidings of support and deliverance! This is the Lord: we have waited for him, and he will save us— This is our God, we have waited for him; we will be glad and rejoice in his salvation.

But you are perhaps ready to exclaim, " O that our Saviour were at hand to " deliver us! He was ever present with " his happy disciples—he was always by " them, to guide them by his wisdom, " to defend them by his power, to pre- " serve and save them by his mercy." Be not faithless, but believing. Your Saviour *is* at hand to deliver you. He is nigh unto all them that call upon him, yea,

yea, all such as call upon him faithfully. Though his dwelling is so high, yet he humbleth himself to behold all those who dwell upon the earth. He is ever present with you, in his word, in his sacraments, in the gifts and graces of his Holy Spirit. You have heard of him by the hearing of the ear—you see him with the eye of faith—during every moment of your existence you are under his protecting care. Even now, as in the time of old, will he fulfil the desire of them that fear him; he will hear their cry, and will help them. When human hopes therefore are abortive, when human succour is inefficient, then lift up your heads with joy—Behold your God! " Look " unto me," he cries, " and be ye saved. " *Be of good cheer* ; *it is I* ; *be not afraid.* " Call upon me in trouble, and I will " deliver you—I will hear you, what " time as the storm falleth upon you."

SERM.
XVIII.

It may be, you are poor and in misery. The world frowns upon you. Want, with all its attendant train of evils, follows closely at your footsteps, and is ready to assail your dwelling. Yet fear not, neither be dismayed. Remember Him who had not where to lay his head. He is favourable to the simple and needy, and he preserveth the souls of the poor. Though you are for a season constrained to struggle with the billows of adversity, yet God is faithful, who, after you have suffered a while, will, in his own time, and according to his own good pleasure, deliver you from all your troubles, and comfort you for the days wherein you have suffered adversity. Meanwhile, let it be the joy of your hearts to remember, that the afflictions which you now suffer were endured by the Lord of all the earth, when he came to bring salvation to his children. While he made his abode among men, he sought not the great, the powerful, and the magnificent,

cent. Though he was rich, for your fakes he became poor, that ye, through his poverty, might be made rich. He preached the gofpel to the poor. The poor were his companions, his friends, his difciples. He exalted the humble and meek. He filled the hungry with good things. The Lord is in his holy temple—the Lord's feat is in heaven; yet his eyes confider the poor. He lifteth the poor out of the duft, he giveth them the exceeding riches of his glory. The word of his mouth is dearer unto them than thoufands of gold and filver. Thus "the poor hath hope," as knowing that he fhall not alway be forgotten, and that the patient abiding of the meek fhall not perifh for ever.

It may be, you are vifited with ficknefs. Difeafe and pain have taken hold upon you. The hand of God is heavy in its chaftifement. All the day long you are troubled, and in the night-feafon you

you take no reft. In the morning you fay, "Would to God it were evening!" and in the evening you fay, "Would to God it were morning!" The trial is grievous, and hard to be borne. It calls for the exertion of all thy faith, and all thy truft in God. If thy delight is not in the Lord, it is true that thou mayft perifh in thy trouble—but, if thy hope is wholly in him, though forrow and anguifh have taken hold upon thee, yet mayft thou rejoice in the Lord; thou mayft joy in the God of thy falvation. Neither adverfity, nor pain, nor ficknefs, nor tribulation, nor death itfelf, fhall be able to feparate you from the love of God, which is in Chrift Jefus our Lord. Whenever therefore you are opprefled with ficknefs, then more efpecially poffefs your fouls in patience—feek after God, and your fouls fhall live. If the ordinary occupations of life, your projects, your defigns (even of good) are retarded by this vifitation, repine not, nor murmur in your hearts. Remember that the business which you are thus called to perform is as necessary as that which you are prevented from performing. You are called to exhibit in your whole conduct the virtues of patient endurance. You are called to suffer something for the SAVIOUR, who suffered so much for you. The afflictions of this present time are not worthy to be compared with the glory that shall be revealed in you. The spirit itself beareth witness with our spirit, that, if we have suffered with Christ, we shall also be glorified together. It is true, that, in the first instance, no chastening is joyous, but grievous; nevertheless, afterwards it brings forth the fruit of peace, and joy, and comfort. Look then, O thou man of sorrows, look unto thy Saviour—behold him stretching forth his hand to help thee! See him, giving medicine to heal thy sickness. Hear him, addressing thee with words of neverfailing comfort,

SERM. XVIII.

fort. "*Be of good cheer—it is I—be not afraid.* I, who during my abode on earth, was myself acquainted with grief—I, whose office it was to bear the afflictions and to remove the sorrows of mankind. I will lift thee up from the gates of death—I will recover thee, and make thee to live—in mercy to thy soul I will deliver thee from the pit of corruption. I am thy God, even the God of whom cometh salvation—I am the Lord, by whom thou shalt escape death. Or, if thou shouldst be called from this fleeting world—if thy soul is now to wing its flight to eternity, I will receive thee to the arms of mercy. I will support thee in thy last conflict. I will ransom thee from the power of death. Let not thine heart be troubled, neither let it be afraid. Hold fast the rejoicing of thy confidence stedfast unto the end. I will call thee, and will welcome thee unto myself, that where I am, there thou mayst be also."

But

But methinks we hear some person cry out, "O that I had only bodily sickness to encounter, then I could well bear it! But I am soul-sick: my spirit is vexed within me, and my heart within me is desolate. I am feeble and sore smitten—I groan for the very disquietness of my heart—God's wrathful displeasure goeth over me—his terrors do I suffer with a troubled mind. Dark and gloomy thoughts take possession of my soul — frightful presages of evil haunt my tortured fancy. I have sinned, O Lord God, I have sinned—I am ashamed, and blush to lift up my face unto thee—my sins have taken such hold upon me that I am not able to look up—yea they are more in number than the hairs of my head, and my heart hath failed me. A terrible voice of most just judgment is continually sounding in my ears. Over my soul is spread an heavy night, an image of that darkness which fear represents as ready to receive me, and yet

yet am I to myself more grievous than the darkness."

What sorrows, what sufferings can be compared to this extremity of anguish ? The spirit of a man may sustain his infirmities, but a wounded spirit who can bear ? For wickedness, condemned by her own witness, is very timorous ; and, being pressed with conscience, always fore-casteth grievous things. Yet is there hope, even in this case, O thou disconsolate sinner. Listen to the voice of thy God! " Come now, saith he, and let us reason together—though your sins be as scarlet, they shall be white as snow— though they be red like crimson, they shall be as wool. JESUS CHRIST DIED ON THE CROSS TO SAVE SINNERS. By his death he made a full, perfect, and sufficient sacrifice, oblation, and satisfaction for the sins of the whole world. Cease to do evil—learn to do well— believe on the Lord Jesus Christ with all thine heart, and be saved."

Thus,

Thus (through the tender mercy of our God) a sense of sin, if it be accompanied with faith and repentance, is speedily followed by the blessed promises of peace and pardon. Scarcely does the offender in the bitterness of his soul cry out, " *O wretched man that I am, who shall deliver me from the body of this death?*" ere he hears the voice of his compassionate Saviour—" Be of good cheer—it is I—I am he that can, and will, deliver you—I, that speak in righteousness, mighty to save." In an instant the tumults of his soul are appeased; he is filled with joy and peace in believing. " I THANK GOD, he joyfully exclaims, *I thank* GOD, *through Jesus Christ our Lord.*"

But perhaps we have trials of a different nature to sustain. Our enemies oppress us, and have us in subjection. Be it so. Others, greater and better than we are, have been called to similar afflictions.

afflictions. Let us reflect how the Royal Prophet, the friend and favourite of his God, was encompassed with an host of enemies — how the floods of ungodly men made him afraid! He cried unto the Lord his God, and gat him to the Lord right humbly. He saw his danger; he saw from whence only he could expect deliverance. "Save me, O God! for the waters are come in even unto my Soul. O deliver me from them that hate me, and from the deep waters—let not the water flood drown me, neither let the deep swallow me up; and let not the pit shut her mouth upon me." Such was his prayer; and the God who heareth prayer gave him an answer of peace. And have *we* then no faith, no hope, no comfort in this sea of troubles, when the tempest of persecution and evil-working rages against us? If we do that which is evil, our fears are natural, and unavoidable. "*Be afraid*, O thou sinner," saith the heavenly monitor,

monitor, "thou hast forsaken thine own mercy. Divine Justice, of which the wicked (though ignorantly and unwillingly) are ever the ministers*, divine justice beareth not the sword in vain." But if, after a full and severe scrutiny (not made lightly, and after the manner of dissemblers) our hearts condemn us not—if we can lift up our eyes with boldness to our God, and recognize his mighty arm in all that befalls us, then may we be of good cheer, and with the ear of faith may hear these divine words—" I, even I, am able to calm the rage and to allay the fury of the oppressor. I, even I, am he that comforteth thee. Who art thou, that thou shouldest be afraid of a man that shall die, and of the son of man, who is as grass, and forgettest the Lord thy

* Psalm xvii. 13. See this passage of Scripture admirably explained and illustrated by the reverend and learned Dr. Goodenough, in his Fast-Sermon preached before the House of Commons, A. D. 1795.

SERM. XVIII.

Redeemer, who maketh the waves of the sea a way for the ransomed to pass over, who hath set a bound to the deep waters of the proud, which they cannot pass, neither turn again to trouble the earth? Though they toss themselves, yet shall they not prevail—though they roar, yet shall they not pass over their appointed limits.

Comforted and sustained by these blessed assurances, the Christian goes on his way rejoicing. Is he *poor?* He is rich in faith. Is he *sick?* His heart is whole in his God. Hath he *sinned* against Heaven? Through the merits of Christ imputed to him, his sins are blotted out. Is he encompassed with *enemies?* He has God for his friend. Stedfastly he pursueth his way, and though storms and tempests arise, yet he believes, and is preserved. When he walks through the valley of the shadow of death, even then he fears no evil; he is not estranged

from

from his hope. Religion, with a voice gracious as that of the angels at the holy sepulchre, never fails to support and animate the hearts of her children. *" Fear not ye; for I know that ye seek Jesus, who was crucified."* Those who were thus employed, neither the darkness of the night, nor the horrors of the tomb, nor the weakness of their sex, nor the danger arising from a barbarous and hostile band of soldiers, could bereave of their intrepidity. A voice from heaven, which spake in thunder to their enemies, and burst the tomb, and sent the trembling astonished guards to flight, THAT VOICE, divested of all its terrors, poured comfort into the afflicted hearts of the pious followers of their Lord, while thus it addressed them: *" Fear not ye; for ye seek Jesus who was crucified!"*

Nor let this blessed admonition be lost upon us. If we seek the crucified Jesus, we shall likewise be devoid of all unholy fear,

fear. Are we even crucified with Christ? Yet shall we live—for if we bear about in our body the dying of the Lord Jesus, then shall the life also of Jesus be made manifest in our body.

The temporary separation of our Saviour from his disciples, and the consequences of that separation, may teach us, that it is the good pleasure of our heavenly Father to make occasional trials of the faith and piety of his servants, even those whom he best loveth, by seeming to withdraw his face from them. Long since hath the prophet spoken of him, as dealing thus with his children: " Verily, *thou art a God that hidest* " *thyself*, O God of Israel, the Saviour." But these severe, however salutary trials, are short in their duration. Soon do we see our Lord approaching to our help, though obstacles present themselves which perhaps appear to us utterly unsurmountable. When the apostles sought for help, and there was none, rather would

would the incarnate God control all the creation, than permit his faithful servants to perish. Though heaven is his throne, and earth his footstool, yet his way is in the sea, and his path in the great waters, and his footsteps are not known.

We see then, that it is of the highest importance both to our present and future happiness, that we should discern our God in the various events of life. A firm persuasion, that his providence directs and orders all things for our ultimate benefit, will not only banish fear from our hearts, but will give us a more abundant measure of hope, and comfort, and joy. Shall we receive good of the Lord, and shall we not receive evil? At his word the stormy wind ariseth—at his word it ceaseth, and there is a calm. Why are we then fearful, but because we are of little faith? Why do we shrink from the inevitable misfortunes of life, but becaufe we do not acknowlege our God in the gloom of adverfity, as well as in the noon-tide fplendour of our profperous fortune?

. In his holy gofpel he hath pointed out to us the methods by which we may feek, and fhall affuredly find, divine confolation. To this let us have recourfe, when we are affailed by fear, or doubt, or forrow. There fhall we hear his voice fupporting and animating us, as it did once his chofen followers. Then fhall we behold our Lord Jefus Chrift, the Author of Salvation, the fountain of hope, the fource of univerfal joy. Our hands will be lifted up in ardent fupplication, befeeching him to fhew the light of his countenance upon his fervants, and to fave us for his mercies fake: and when we make our prayer unto him he will hear us. " The Lord of Hofts is with us, the God of Jacob is our refuge. Sing unto the Lord a new fong, song, for he hath done marvellous things. Sing unto the Lord, praise his name, be telling of his salvation from day to day. God is our hope and strength; a very present help in trouble. Therefore will we not fear, though the earth be removed, and though the hills be carried into the midst of the sea—though the waters thereof rage and swell—though the mountains shake at the tempest of the same. THE LORD OF HOSTS IS WITH US, THE GOD OF JACOB IS OUR REFUGE.

SERMON

SERMON XIX.

THE CHRISTIAN'S REST.

SERMON XIX.

THE CHRISTIAN'S REST.

PSALM iii. 5.

I laid me down and slept—I awaked, for the Lord sustained me.

THE words now read to you have a natural, and they have a spiritual signification. They are a morning hymn for the faithful Christian while on earth; and they will, on the resurrection-day, burst

burst from his joyful heart, after his silence in the grave. "*I laid me down and slept—I awaked, for the Lord sustained me!*"

My discourse will necessarily follow the track thus pointed out to it. And I shall speak of sleep, and of waking—of death, and of rising again.

It is much to be lamented, that mankind in general neither feel nor acknowlege, as they ought, the blessings bestowed upon them by the indulgent Providence of God, till his divine correction awakens them to gratitude and duty—that they know not how to appreciate the kindness of the Giver, till it pleases him, by some severe, but just visitation, to withdraw the gift. Amongst these obvious, but ill-requited mercies, I fear we may often enumerate the comforts of *Health*—of *Ease*, or exemption from pain—and of *Sleep*, that seasonable refreshment

freshment of our weak and exhausted powers. Nor can there be a more evident proof of the mercy of our heavenly Father, than his permitting us for a time to be deprived of these his gracious gifts, that so we may learn to be less insensible of his favours when we again enjoy them. Thus, when we are brought low by sickness, we then best know the inestimable value of health, and pour forth our hearts in prayer to God for its return. When we are tortured with pain, we remember the days of ease and comfort which have been many, and wonder, that we were not more sensible of former mercies vouchsafed to us. When we have passed a sleepless night, waking either through indisposition, or anxiety, then do we consider the hours of refreshment (hours of unheeded and unacknowleged mercy) when rest was afforded to our wearied bodies, and relaxation to the powers of the mind—when we awaked, and beheld, and our sleep was sweet unto us.

Let

Let us, however, carefully diftinguifh between the proper enjoyment, and the ungrateful abufe of any gift of God. When we fpeak of the benefits of moderate *reft*, we muft not be mifunderftood, as if we were recommending floth and luxury. When God gives his beloved fleep, he would have all the active powers of the foul invigorated by this precious boon—when the day has dawned, and the fhadows are fled away, he would have man rife up to his work and to his labour unto the evening. And then it is his will, that, " wearied with labours and cares of the day, we fhould come to our God for quiet and repofe, and for new fupplies of ftrength to drooping nature"—that when we have been thus refrefhed, we may afterwards awake, better qualified to fet forth his praifes, and to devote ourfelves to his fervice *.

* See Bifhop Andrews's "Evening Devotions," tranflated from he original Greek by Dean Stanhope.

In a grateful sense of our continued preservation, and of the tender mercies of God, which are renewed with every opening day, let us take the wings of the morning, and in heart and mind ascend to Heaven. Let our first accents be the accents of praise, when we find ourselves, (by the divine goodness), awakened, as it were, to new life, and enabled to perform the several duties of the day which it has pleased God to add to our lives. *I laid me down, and slept,* saith the Psalmist; *I awaked, sustained by* the Providence of *God.*

Thus much for the words of my text in their literal signification. We proceed to examine them, as applicable to that sleep from which we shall not awake, till the morning dawns that never shall have a night—till the voice of the archangel, and the trumpet of God, summons us from the tomb[*].

[*] 1 Thess. iv. 16.

SERM. XIX.

The intimate connection between sleep and death has been the theme of every writer, from the earliest period of time, who has had occasion to speak of either. The divine biographers in particular, after having recorded the actions of any distinguished character, close the narrative in one and the same simple but interesting form of words—" He slept with his fathers." And what comparison can be more apposite ? what parallel can be drawn with more exactness ? The one is a deprivation of those powers and faculties, of which the other is only a cessation for the time. In other words, sleep is a temporary death ; and death *(as far as this world is concerned)* is a perpetual sleep. And as the faithful servant of God closes his eyes in slumber, when the night cometh, trusting that the divine Providence will preserve him unto the morning, so when he is called upon to

leave

leave the world, he closes his eyes in death, committing the guardianship of his soul to Him on whom he hath believed, and being perſuaded, that he will *keep ſafe that which is committed to him, and will raiſe it up at the laſt day* *.

Let us then carry on this alluſion, by enquiring into thoſe cauſes which tend to produce quiet and comfortable ſleep; and let us ſee whether they will not all of them apply themſelves to our departure from life, and whether they will not tend to make that likewiſe quiet and comfortable.

In the firſt place, he who would obtain ſweet and undiſturbed ſleep muſt be in *Charity* with all the world. Revenge and malice, envy and hatred, plant thorns under the pillow; while

* 2 Tim. i. 12.

SERM. XIX.

the friend of mankind, who neither feareth evil from others, nor deviseth mischief in his own heart, enjoys pure and uninterrupted repose. In like manner, he, who expects to awake the companion of Angels, must possess an angelic disposition when he goeth to his long sleep. Love and peace sustain the expiring soul—and direct the hopes of the dying Christian to those regions of blessedness, where the Angels, and Spirits of just men made perfect, are united in bonds of everlasting Charity.

A second requisite for bodily rest, is *A calm and untroubled soul.* The world and worldly thoughts, we all know, too often disturb our repose. It is not sufficient if we devote our day to this tyrannous master; he would likewise deprive us of our slumbers. But let us once arrive at that happy serenity, which leads us to resign all worldly concerns to the care of a good Providence, then,

under

under a sense of the divine protection, we shall each of us cry out—" *I will lay me down in peace, and take my rest—for it is thou, Lord, only, which makest me dwell in safety* *. The departing Soul must likewise be purified from all undue attachment to mortality, if it would be prepared for a quiet resignation of itself into the hands of its Creator and Redeemer. When the messenger of death approaches, when we behold him pointing to the throne of Judgement, where will be then the dreams of this vain life? *All those things shall pass away like a shadow, and no trace shall be left by which they may be found* †.

A third cause of quiet repose, which perhaps, indeed, might with propriety have been placed in the first rank, is *Innocence*. The mind, labouring under a sense of unrepented guilt,

* Psalm iv.—8.   † Wisd. v.—9.

SERM. seeks in vain for that sleep which
XIX. God is graciously pleased to bestow on
those whom he loveth. The sinner, who
has fled into society for refuge — who
has stifled by affected merriment the re-
monstrances of his own heart, during
the day, is now, at the solemn hour of
night, left to the severe reproaches of
that inward monitor. Terrors now return upon him with redoubled force.
His CONSCIENCE, like the pale spectre,
which the eye of superstition forms to
itself in the midnight hour, scares him
with visions of horrible darkness, and
the alarm drives slumber far away from
him. Or if he sleep, he is tortured by
the tumultuous workings of his fancy,
more fearful than the thoughts of the
righteous can picture to themselves.
Sleeping or waking, *"There is no peace,"
saith my God," to the wicked." They are like
the troubled sea*, in a state of perpetual
agitation and disquiet. Whereas, the

* Isaiah 57.—21.   ver. 20.

righteou

righteous goeth to his bed, with the difposition he shall one day go to his grave. His reflections on the past day present objects of peace and comfort to his mind—services, imperfect indeed, but such as the divine goodness will deign to accept. Having endeavoured to bring every thought into the obedience of Christ—having directed his words to the use of edifying, and having framed all his actions with a view to the glory and praise of God, he resteth in peace, firmly relying on the mercy of Heaven. Faith attends him to his repose, and Piety is the Guardian Angel that hovers over his head. As to the reflections of the dying sinner, let the minister of the gospel, whose painful duty it is to attend him in the last scene of expiring nature, let the minister of the gospel speak, and, without disguise or palliation, let him deliver a narrative, full of terror indeed, but full of instruction. Let him give a portrait of death, armed with his

SERM. XIX.

his envenomed sting, and triumphing over his miserable victim. By his own heart the sinner is convicted; by his mouth he is condemned. The night is come upon him; his work is unperformed. There is neither wisdom nor understanding, nor knowlege, nor counsel, nor repentance, nor faith, nor hope, in the grave, whither he is immediately descending. Nothing but a miracle of divine mercy can prevent the sentence of guiltiness from proceeding against him. Nothing remains, but a certain fearful looking-for of judgment and fiery indignation, which shall devour the enemies of God. O that men were wise, that they would consider these things, that they would seek peace and reconciliation with the Almighty!

Further. No sleep can be quiet or salutary, if the party be not in a state of *health*. For if debauchery or intemperance hath impaired the constitution,

then

then *the earthly body presseth down the soul**, and undisturbed rest is sought for in vain. Let us hear the sentiments of the Roman poet upon this occasion—and while we hear them, let us admire the power of Him, who at his pleasure can make truth, and virtue, and good counsel, proceed from the most unhallowed lips. "The body," saith Horace, " burthened with the vices of the " preceding day, by its weight bows " down the soul along with it, and fixes " to the ground a portion of the breath " of God." Now if bodily health is indispensably necessary to our tasting in all its sweetness the blessing of untroubled repose, it is equally essential to the serenity of our closing hours, that we should hold fast the form of sound words, and adhere stedfastly to all things which the servant of God should know and believe, *to his soul's health*. We must be strong in the faith: and Christianity, true, genu-

---

* Wisd. ix. 15.

ine, vital Christianity, must possess and animate our hearts, be our outward frame never so feeble. " There is no " rational principle, by which a man " can die contented, but a trust in the " mercy of God, through the merits of " Jesus Christ." Strengthened by this pious confidence we shall rest in peace; sustained by the arm of our Redeemer we shall lie down, and our sleep shall be sweet.

The last particular which I shall mention, as conducive to rest, is *Labour*. Indeed the one word in some measure implies the other. Rest from inaction is an absurdity. Now the sleep of a labouring man is sweet; but indolence is the bane of repose. He who is preparing for his grave, will in like manner possess his soul in far more tranquillity, if his life has been useful, active, and beneficent, than the selfish, sordid wretch, whose only occupation

has

has been to consult his own ease and pleasure, and who to these unworthy pursuits has dedicated his time, his faculties, all those noble endowments, which God hath given to man. Our blessed Lord, in his last discourse to his disciples, addresses his Father in terms to this effect: *"I have glorified thy name upon earth—I have* FINISHED THE WORK *which thou gavest me to do, and now receive me to thyself**.—The dying Christian who " has served his generation by the will of God" may, without presumption, use the same words—and faith will represent his Saviour as calling him to the glory purchased for those, who have employed themselves, with zeal and fidelity, in his service.

The requisites then to rest, whether in our bed or in our grave, are CHARITY, PEACE, INNOCENCE, HEALTH, (in one case bodily, in the other spiritual),

* John xvii.—4.

and

and Labour. Allow me to add, that he who commits himself to his repose without offering up his prayers to the Almighty, cannot with reason complain, if it should please the Almighty to withdraw his protection from him. "Sleep," saith an eminent writer, "is so like death, "that I dare not trust it, without saying "my prayers." Am I addressing any person, who, from carelessness, indifference, or from any other still more culpable motive, lives in the habitual neglect of this solemn, sacred, indispensable duty? If so, let me propose these questions seriously to him, and let his own heart make the reply. *" What security hast thou, O man, that " this night thy soul will not be required " of thee?* When thou goest to sleep, " how canst thou tell, that thou shalt " ever wake again? Wert thou actually " on thy death-bed, wouldst not thou " wish to close thy life with prayer? " Wouldst thou not offer supplication " to the Almighty, that he would receive

" thy

"thy foul to mercy? Wouldſt thou
"not endeavour to prepare thyſelf for
"that awful hour, which is to uſher thee
"into a new and myſterious ſtate of
"being? When God calleth thee, wilt
"thou not be aſhamed to ſay, thou haſt
"not made thyſelf ready? Conſider
"earneſtly, how little, in the hour of
"death, and in the day of judgment,
"ſuch feigned excuſes will avail before
"God!"

Remember what I ſay, and may the Lord give you underſtanding in all things! Think not, that the offices of piety bring with them any degree of gloom or deſpondency. Think not, that the faithful ſervant of God (who, by prayer and the exerciſes of devotion, prepares himſelf for the hour of his departure), is excluded from the enjoyment of thoſe bleſſings, which a God of mercy hath beſtowed on his creatures. On the contrary, while he looks to heaven for the fulneſs

SERM. XIX.

fulness of joy, he is so far from being a stranger to earthly happiness, that he is the sole, the exclusive, possessor of it, in its unsullied purity. But still his loins are girded about, and his lamp is burning; and he is himself as one who waiteth for his Lord, that, when he cometh and knocketh, he may open to him immediately.

It is want of faith alone, which makes us shrink back with horror from the thought of dissolution. If we believe aright the words of sacred truth, we most assuredly know, that the Christian, who *liveth* in peace with God and man, *dieth* likewise in peace, and sleepeth quietly in his tomb, a happy candidate for immortality. For the time shall most assuredly come—the voice of God hath foretold it—when that departed Christian, nay when that his mouldered body now sleeping in the dust, shall arise to a new life, a life not to be succeeded again

again by death. Then shall he awake, through God who calleth, through Christ who redeemeth, through the blessed Spirit who strengtheneth him. He shall awake, lively, joyful, active, his powers invigorated and restored, as he had been accustomed to awake while on earth, when Peace and Devotion had given sweetness to his rest. As then his earliest thoughts were addressed to Heaven, so now he welcomes his eternal day with a song of praise. "Awake, awake, O my Soul, from thy sleep. The morning of the resurrection dawns—the shadows of mortality fly away. Lift up your heads, O ye gates—I, even I, with my brethren and companions, the redeemed of God, shall enter in. My body, which was sown in corruption, is raised in incorruption. It was sown in weakness—it is raised in power. It was sown in dishonour—it is raised in glory. *I laid me down and slept, I awaked—for the Lord sustained me.*"

SERMON

SERMON XX.

THE CHRISTIAN'S GLORY.

(Preached on All-Saints'-Day.)

SERMON XX.

THE CHRISTIAN'S GLORY.

HEBREWS xii.—22, 23, 24.

Ye are come unto Mount Sion, and unto the city of the Living God, the heavenly Jerusalem; and to an innumerable company of Angels,
To the general Assembly and Church of the first-born, which are written in Heaven, and to God the Judge of all, and to the spirits of just men made perfect,
And to JESUS, *the Mediator of the new Covenant.*

BY faith we behold this glory, which shall be revealed—by faith, whose just prerogative it is, to represent the promises

mises of God, which shall hereafter receive their due completion, as even now fulfilling in behalf of his people; and as far as intellectual enjoyments can reach, they are indeed fulfilling: while the soul dwells with rapture on that bright and glorious prospect, which exhibits mortality as swallowed up of life.

In the words of my text the inspired writer points out the blessed and happy state of those, who, having fought a good fight, having finished their course, and having kept the faith, are admitted into the kingdom of their Father. After directing the attention of his converts to those denunciations of vengeance, proclaimed by a God of justice, amidst the majestic horrors of Sinai, he proceeds to describe the covenant of mercy made with us by a divine Mediator, by virtue of which we are assured, "that God hath not appointed us unto wrath, but to obtain salvation through our Lord Jesus Christ."

The Christian's Glory.

Chrift." At the promulgation of the Law, the earth trembled and quaked—the foundations alfo of the hills moved and were fhaken at the prefence of God, becaufe he was wroth*. The mountain burned with fire—clouds and thick darknefs overfhadowed the reft of the world—a mighty tempeft was ftirred up round about—the Lord thundered out of heaven, and the higheft gave his thunder—while the found of a trumpet, waxing louder and louder, was fucceeded by a voice too dreadful for the mortal ear to fupport; the voice of HIM, who declares himfelf to be GOD of gods, and LORD of lords, a great God, a mighty and a terrible. At the manifeftation of the *Gofpel*, when the glory of the

---

* יגיד עליו רעו
מקנה אף על עולה:

The noife thereof (i. e. of the thunder) fheweth concerning HIM, *that he poffeffeth wrath becaufe of iniquity*; fee Job, xxxvi. 32. If any Hebrew MS. or printed copy authorized the fubftitution of רעמו for רעו the fenfe would be more perfect, and the connection of the fenfe with chap. xxxvi. 32, and chap. xxxvii. 1. would more evidently appear.

SERM.
XX.
Lord shone round about those to whom Christ was first revealed, an angel was sent from heaven to dispel from their minds all terror and consternation: " *Fear not,*" saith the messenger of love and mercy, " Fear not; for, behold, I bring you good tidings of great joy." A multitude of the heavenly host confirmed the gracious words; they ascribed glory to God, proclaimed PEACE on earth, and announced good-will towards men. Former things then passed away, all things became new—and God reconciled a sinful world unto himself through Christ Jesus, who was the end of the Law, and the fulness of the Gospel. " By Him all that believe are now justified from all things from which they could not be justified by the law of Moses." Through His all-sufficient merits, through His all-prevailing intercession, our unworthy services are accepted, our sins are blotted out, the arms of mercy are extended to repentant man. Now then

we

we are no more strangers and foreigners, but fellow-citizens with the saints, and of the houshold of God. We are built upon the foundation of the apostles and prophets, Jesus Christ himself being the head corner-stone. We look on the regions of peace and glory as our own bright reversion, our promised inheritance, our haven of everlasting rest. Thus, though the law made nothing perfect, the bringing in of a better hope did: through which hope we draw nigh unto God *.

I. Through faith then we have evidence of those things which shall hereafter be accomplished, but which are too transcendently glorious for "the sense of human sight." Through faith we see Heaven opened. We see Jesus, *the Mediator of the new covenant*, crowned with majesty and honour. We behold *an innumerable company of angels*, surrounding the throne of glory.

* Heb. vii. 19.

The spirits of juft men made perfect, the general affembly and church of the firft-born, whofe names are written in heaven, fing the high praifes of God, *the Judge of all,* " who hath tranflated them to the kingdom of his dear Son, in whom they have redemption, through his blood." Through faith we hear the voice, which introduces us, as it were, into the manfions of the bleffed. " *Ye* ARE COME *unto Mount Sion, the city of the living God,* THE HEAVENLY JERUSALEM."

Such is the high prize of our calling—for the attainment of which we are directed to lay afide every weight, and the fins which do fo eafily befet us, and to run with patience the race that is fet before us, looking unto Jefus, THE AUTHOR AND FINISHER OF OUR FAITH, who for our fake endured the crofs, and is now on the right-hand of the throne of God. Through him alone we obtain remiffion of our fins—we are filled with
the

the hope of glory—and are made partakers of the inheritance of the faints in light.

Bleffed are they, O Lord God of hofts, who fhall be called to their reft in the heavenly Jerufalem, the city of the Great King! Bleffed are they whom thou chufeft,' and receiveft unto thyfelf! They fhall dwell in thy courts; and fhall be fatisfied with the pleafures of thine houfe, even of thy holy temple. Of the peculiar nature of that bleffednefs which they fhall enjoy we can form no adequate idea: it is not neceffary—it is not poffible, that we fhould. We know in part only; we fee but as through a glafs darkly*. Mortal perceptions are not equal to the comprehending immortal felicity. Hardly do we guefs aright at things that are upon earth; and with labour do we find the things that are before us: as for the things that are in heaven, who hath

---

* ἐν αἰνίγματι. 1 Cor. xiii. 12.

fearched

SERM. XX.

searched them out? But this we know, that it is a state of perfect, of never-ceasing HAPPINESS—happiness, unalloyed by sorrow, unchecked by fear or solicitude—pure and divine happiness, worthy of the God who gives it, worthy of the Saviour who hath purchased it for us by his most precious blood. This we know; and, believing, we rejoice with joy unspeakable and full of glory. We presume not, we wish not to enquire farther. Enough knowlege is imparted to us, to call forth our utmost exertions, to animate our zeal, and give ardour to our obedience. Enough is imparted, to support us under the sufferings of this present life, and to raise our affections from earth to heaven, where the God of glory reigneth in the midst of his saints. When we dwell in contemplations like these, our souls thirst for God, for the living God: " When shall we come," (we are ready to exclaim) " when shall " we come, and appear before our God?
" In

" In his presence is the fulness of joy—at
" his right-hand there is pleasure for
" evermore."

To what portion of their glorious reward the righteous * are admitted immediately after their dissolution, and what part of it is reserved for the day of final recompence—these are questions on which it becoms us not to dwell with too minute investigation. Whither shall we go for information on this awful subject, when the Holy Spirit hath veiled it in mysterious silence? Let it suffice us, that God is our God for ever and ever—that he is not only our guide *unto* death, but *in* death, and *after* death—that he is the God of our fathers, the God of Abraham,

---

* The author hopes it is scarcely necessary to observe, that by the word righteous, as used in this sense, he means those, to whose repentance, faith, and obedience, *the saving righteousness of Jesus Christ* is imputed: for by Him ALONE we obtain remission of our sins, and are made partakers of the kingdom of heaven.

ham, of Isaac, and of Jacob, the God of the spirits of all flesh—that blessed are the dead, which die in the Lord—that the souls of the righteous, from the time that they leave their earthly tabernacles, are in the hands of God—that though in the sight of the unwise they may seem to die, and their departure may be taken for misery, yet they are in peace—that the great apostle testified his " vehement desire" to be absent from the body, *and to be present with the Lord**—and that Jesus Christ, the Author of life and mercy, when he was placed as a victim on the altar of his cross, spake thus to the dying penitent beside him: " This day shalt thou be with " me in Paradise." For the rest, O Lord, we tarry thy leisure: our hearts are comforted, for we put our trust in thee. With thee do live the spirits of them that depart hence in the Lord. With thee the souls of the faithful, after they are delivered from

* 2 Cor. v. 6.

the

the burden of the flesh, are in joy and felicity. Thou wilt keep them safe that are committed to thy charge, till the number of thine elect being accomplished, they shall have their PERFECT CONSUMMATION of bliss, both in body and soul, in thine eternal glory.

II. Having described the place of the tabernacle of the Most High, unto which the ransomed of the Lord shall be translated after their earthly warfare, the words of inspiration next point out who shall be their associates. *" Ye are come to an innumerable company of* ANGELS." Those pure and holy beings, the sons of God, the morning stars * of heaven—those celestial guardians, who once, by divine appointment, watched over, succoured, defended us on earth—who once, as ministers of God's good providence, were our unseen protectors

* See Job, xxxviii. 7.

against

against unseen dangers, encamping round about us, and delivering us—those spirits of love, and peace, and holiness, who rejoiced at our conversion, and shared our triumphs over the powers of darkness, shall then bear witness to our admission into the regions of joy, and shall welcome us as fellow-heirs of everlasting felicity.

Here let us pause a moment, while we reflect on the nature of this astonishing privilege. Shall we, who are born in sin, and the children of wrath—shall the fallen offspring of fallen parents receive such a measure of heavenly grace, as to become worthy of that joy which is the portion of angels?—angels, who never sinned, never fell, never by disobedience forfeited the blessings which their Creator bestowed on them? Lord, what is man, that thou hast such respect unto him; or the son of man, that thou so regardest him?—that in thine abundant

dant mercy thou haft delivered him from the bondage of corruption, and haft called him to the habitations of joy, to the fociety of angels, to the glorious liberty of the children of God? Yet fuch are the wonders which thou haft wrought for us; and for this caufe will we give thanks unto thee for ever, and fhew forth thy praife from generation to generation. For this caufe, with angels and arch-angels, and with all the company of heaven, we laud and magnify thy glorious name, evermore praifing thee and faying, Holy, holy, holy, Lord God of hofts! Thou art worthy, O Lord, to receive glory, and honour, and power! Glory be to thee, O Lord moft High!

III. And lo, a voice proceeds from the everlafting throne, which calls on the *faints of God* to add their hallelujahs to the ftrains of angels. "Praife your God, all ye his fervants, and ye that fear him,

him, both small and great." At the divine mandate, the glorious company of the apostles, the goodly fellowship of the prophets, the noble army of martyrs, all other servants of the once suffering, but now glorified, Messiah, fall down and worship Him that sitteth upon the throne, saying, " Amen! Hallelu-
" jah! Worthy art thou, O Lord, to
" take the book, and to open the seals
" thereof; for thou wast slain, and hast
" redeemed us to God by thy blood."
And again, a voice is heard, as it were the voice of a great multitude, and as the voice of many waters, and as the voice of mighty thunderings, saying,
" *Hallelujah, for the Lord God omnipotent*
" *reigneth! let us be glad and rejoice, and*
" *give honour unto Him!*" Thus doth THE GENERAL ASSEMBLY AND CHURCH OF THE FIRST-BORN, WHICH ARE WRITTEN IN HEAVEN, shew forth the honour of God, and make his praise to be glorious.

But

But the heirs of immortality are taught to aspire to a degree of bliss, still more sublime, still more sacred, than that which results from the society of saints and angels. They will behold the presence of God in righteousness. They will see Him; as He is. " Ye are come," saith the prophetic language of inspiration, " ye are come to God, THE JUDGE OF ALL." Here language fails—and here imagination, which should supply its place, fails likewise. Silent adoration, gratitude unutterable, reverential love, these fill the whole soul of man, when he remembers the gracious promise, which tells him, that, if he is pure in heart, he shall see God*.

Encouraged by this " earnest of their future inheritance," the blessed Saints of old were more than conquerors, amidst the calamities which it was their portion to sustain. They had trials of cruel mockings

---

* Matthew, v.—8.

mockings and scourgings—of bonds and imprisonment—they were stoned—were sawn asunder—were tempted—were slain with the sword—they were destitute, afflicted, tormented: but in all their sufferings here upon earth they cherished in their hearts the promise of that blessed hour, when the glory of Christ should appear, and when they should be glad also with exceeding joy. They remembered the words of the Lord Jesus, how he said, " Father, I will that they whom thou hast given me be with me where I am, that they may behold the glory which thou hast given me." Sure that the divine will would have its full accomplishment, and that the day was near in its approach, when they should behold the presence of God, they *gloried* in tribulation—they *took pleasure* in infirmities, in reproaches, in distresses. " We know," said one of the first and greatest of these true heroes, " we know that if our earthly house of this tabernacle

nacle were diffolved, we have a building of God, an houfe not made with hands, eternal in the heavens. For in this we groan, earneftly defiring to be clothed upon with our houfe which is from Heaven."

V. With fuch examples as thefe before his eyes, the Chriftian preffes forward to the mark, as one that ftriveth for the maftery. He runs, not as uncertainly. He regulates all his actions, his words, his thoughts, with reference to the confummation of all things. He lifts up his eyes to the everlafting hills, where the God of mercy reigneth, praying always with all prayer and fupplication, and watching thereunto with all perfeverance, that he may be conducted by the divine counfel while he is on earth, and that hereafter he may join that bleffed fociety, where THE SPIRITS OF JUST MEN MADE PERFECT are partakers of everlafting glory. Then fhall he behold thofe those great and illustrious saints of God, on whose virtues he has meditated with delight, whose labours, whose example, whose writings, have conduced to keep alive his faith and piety, his zeal and devotion, his hope and charity. Then with patriarchs and prophets, apostles, evangelists, confessors, martyrs, all those who have served their God faithfully from the beginning of time, he shall rejoice with unspeakable joy. How are our hearts comforted, how are they elevated by the thought, that we, and all those who have the fondest place in our affections, shall, if we live in the faith of God, and depart in his fear, be most blessed to all eternity!—that we shall *together* be made partakers of the kingdom of our God, and the glory of his Christ, who hath opened the gates of Heaven to all believers! In what manner, and to what extent these hopes will be realized, He only knows, who hath decreed that the soul shall

shall one day be reunited to the body, and shall be received into the mansions of immortality: but that they *will* be realized, who can doubt, who has ever felt the endearing ties which are formed by filial, parental, or conjugal love? Is it to be supposed, that the Almighty hath implanted in our souls these exquisite feelings to be so soon interrupted, so soon, as it were, annihilated?—feelings that, instead of the blessing, would be the torment of our lives, did the sad thought of a total separation from all that we delight in arise to embitter every enjoyment? But in the sure and certain hope of future restoration to the beloved friends who go before us, we resign them, though not without poignant sorrow, at least without despair. We consider them as gone on a journey, whither we ourselves shall ere long follow them—and though this temporary separation should be fatal to the survivor's earthly happiness, yet faith antici-

pates

SERM. XX.

pates the blessed day, when we shall meet again, to be separated no more—when, in the presence of that God, with whom is the fulness of everlasting joy, love, and doubtless social love, shall reign, without alloy, and without interruption—when, in that state of bliss which is purchased for us by the precious blood of Christ, and to which we shall be guided by the Holy Ghost, the COMFORTER, we shall be restored to the objects of our love, once more, and for ever.

VI. Lastly, it is appointed to the blessed in Heaven, to behold JESUS, THE MEDIATOR OF THE NEW COVENANT—the covenant of mercy, by which sinful men were restored to those privileges which they had forfeited, and to the favour of that God whom they had offended. They will behold him, on the throne of his co-eternal Father, King of kings, and Lord of lords. " Rejoice greatly, O daughter

O daughter of Zion; shout, O daughter of Jerusalem—Behold, thy King reigneth! He is great, and clothed with Majesty; he sitteth between the Cherubim; he is encompassed with ineffable glory." Hosannahs to the Son of God now fill the heaven of heavens. He it is, who hath purchased this eternal inheritance for his saints by the shedding of his most precious blood, *the blood of the covenant.* He is the door, by which they shall enter into that city, whose builder and maker is God. He shall confess before the company of angels, and shall acknowlege as his own, all his faithful servants, who, while they were on earth, confessed HIM before men. He shall exalt them to everlasting glory—he shall make them equal unto the angels. He, who is the great High Priest of his triumphant Church, shall bring his redeemed into the holy of holies, and shall present them faultless before the presence of his Father, with exceeding joy.

SERM.
XX.
joy. He, to whose human nature all power was given both in heaven and earth, shall see his chosen flock accepted before God, the Maker of all things, and Judge of all men, who shall receive the spirits of the just—those spirits whom he hath proved, and found worthy of himself. The Lord Christ Jesus shall perfect for ever them that are sanctified; not weighing their merits, but pardoning their offences, and clothing them with the garments of his righteousness. He shall bring the ransomed of the Lord with songs, and with everlasting joy upon their heads—he shall conduct them into the courts of the Lord's house, even into the midst of thee, O Jerusalem.

But who shall ascend into the hill of the Lord? Who shall rise up in his holy place? They, who have clean hands, and pure hearts—they, who by faith and patience strive to inherit the promises—they, who cleanse themselves
from

from all filthiness of the flesh and spirit, perfecting holiness in the fear of the Lord—they, who endeavour with every power and faculty of their souls, to follow the example of their Saviour, and to be made like unto him. They, who by humility, by meekness, by innocence, by sanctity, by love unfeigned, approve themselves as the disciples of Christ. They, who use the means of grace, as conducive to the hope of glory. They, who frame and fashion their lives in obedience to the will of God, so that faith worketh with their works, and by works their faith is made perfect. They, even they, shall receive the blessing from the Lord, and righteousness from the God of their salvation. They shall rejoice because their names are written in heaven. These shall ascend into the hill of the Lord. These shall rise up in his holy place. While they walked in the steps of their Redeemer on earth, he saw them from the habitation of his holiness,

and

and of his glory—he faw, and was well pleafed. While they fpake of the things pertaining to the kingdom of God, he hearkened, and heard it, and a book of remembrance was written before him for them that feared the Lord, and that thought upon his name. "They fhall "be mine, faith the Lord of hofts, in " that day when I make up my jewels; " and I will fpare them, as a man fpareth " his own fon that ferveth him."

We fee our calling, brethren. O let us remember that the time is fhort, and that the work appointed us to perform is of inexpreffible importance—that there is but a ftep between us and death— and that at our diffolution, we fhall be configned either to the habitations of endlefs forrow, to the fociety of devils and tormented fpirits, or to the fellow- fhip of ALL SAINTS, to the reft which remaineth for the people of God. The bright reward, the glorious inheritance of of life eternal is not offered to the rebellious and obdurate, to the carelefs and indifferent, to the licentious and profane. Thefe follow the multitude to do evil; they purfue the broad path which leadeth to deftruction: whereas ftrait is the gate, and narrow is the way which leadeth unto life, and few there be that find it. They only who look for their God in *holinefs*, fhall behold his power and glory—for *them* is laid up the crown of righteoufnefs, which the Lord, the righteous Judge, hath promifed to all them that love his appearing.

We praife thee therefore, O God; we acknowlege thee to be the Lord. Thine is the greatnefs, and the glory, and the victory and the Majefty. In thine hand s power and might, and in thine hand it is to make great, and to give ftrength unto all. All thy Saints fhall give thanks unto thee, even the fouls whom thou haft redeemed. The general affembly and

SERM. XX.

and Church of the firft-born who are written in heaven shall worship thee, yea, they shall sing of thee, and praife thy name. "Through thee, O bleſſed "Jefus," they will rapturoufly exclaim, " through thee we are come to the city " of the living God, the mount Zion, " the heavenly Jerufalem; for thy " mercy endureth for ever. Through " thee we are made the companions of " angels; for thy mercy endureth for " ever. Through thy mediation we are " admitted into the prefence of God the " Judge of all; for thy mercy endureth " for ever. Through thee we are reckon- " ed among the number of the fpirits of " juft men made perfect; for thy mercy " endureth for ever. Thou haft fulfilled " thy gracious promife to thy Church, " and having fhed on it the bright beams. " of thy light during its warfare, thou " haft at length exalted it to the light of " everlafting life; for thy mercy endur- " eth for ever. Therefore we will rejoice " in the contemplation of thy glory; we
" will

"will praife thee, we will blefs thee, we will adore thee to all eternity."

Let thy name, O bleffed Jefus, be confeffed on earth, as it is in heaven! for through thy name alone can we hope to obtain falvation. Of ourfelves we can do no good thing; but we can do all things, if thou wilt ftrengthen us. Sanctify us, O Lord, by thy Spirit; feed and ftrengthen us by thy body; ranfom us from our fins by thy blood! We truft in thee; let us never be confounded. We come unto thee; receive us unto thyfelf. Receive us—and " make us to be numbered with thy faints in glory everlafting!"

Now to FATHER, SON, and HOLY GHOST, three divine Perfons, and one eternal GOD, be afcribed, as is moft due, by the Church militant on earth, and the Church triumphant in Heaven, all honour, power, adoration, and praife, now, and for evermore! Amen.

FINIS.

Published, by the same Author,

I. CONTEMPLATIONS ON THE SACRED HISTORY, ALTERED FROM THE WORKS OF BISHOP HALL, in four Volumes. (12mo.) 1793.

II. The Universal Remedy in Time of Affliction. From Bishop Hall's Works. (12mo.) 1796.

III. ΚΑΡΑΚΤΑΚΟΣ ΕΠΙ ΜΩΝΗ: sive, Cl. Masoni Caractacus, Græco Carmine redditus: Cum Versione Latinâ. (8vo.) 1781.

IV. ΣΑΜΨΩΝ ΑΓΩΝΙΣΤΗΣ. Joannis Miltoni Samson Agonistes, Græco Carmine redditus: Cum Versione Latinâ. (8vo.) 1788.

V. A Sermon preached before the Governors of the Magdalen-Hospital. (4to.) 1788.

VI. A Sermon preached before the Guardians of the Asylum for Helpless Orphans. (4to.) 1791.

VII. A Sermon preached in the Parish Church of Hanwell, in behalf of the French Emigrant Clergy. (4to.) 1793.

VIII. The same, in French, published by desire of the Bishop of St. Pol de Leon. (8vo.) 1794.

IX. A

IX. A Sermon preached in the Parifh Church of St. Martin in the Fields, at the Vifitation of the Right Reverend Father in God, Beilby, Lord Bifhop of London. (4to.) 1794.

X. A Narrative of Facts, printed at Bruffels, fuppofed to throw Light on the Hiftory of the Briftol-Maniac: Tranflated from the French, and infcribed to Mifs Hannah More. (12mo.) 1786.

XI. Extracts from the Old Verfion of the Pfalms of David, felected for the Ufe of the Parifh-Church of Hanwell in the County of Middlefex. (12mo.) 3d Edition. 1791.

www.ingramcontent.com/pod-product-compliance
Lightning Source LLC
Chambersburg PA
CBHW032009300426
44117CB00008B/953